Essay

and letter writing

L. G. ALEXANDER

LONGMAN

LONGMAN GROUP LIMITED
London

Associated companies, branches and representatives
throughout the world

First published 1965
New impressions *1965; *1966 (twice);
*1968; *1969; *1970 (twice);
*1972; *1973; *1974;
*1975; 1977

ISBN 0 582 52303 6

Printed in Singapore by
Kyodo-Shing Loong Printing Industries Pte Ltd

Contents

Part 2

Foreword

THE AIM OF THIS BOOK is to provide the overseas teacher and student with a wide variety of suitable material for essay work and letter-writing, together with simple instructions on how to go about it. The subject-matter is so arranged that the student will be able to work systematically at the *writing* of English over a long period. The teacher, too, will have at his disposal a great number of exercises and topics so that he can keep a close check on the written work of his pupils.

The first chapter presupposes that the student has covered the main difficulties in elementary grammar and has acquired a limited active vocabulary, without actually having had any experience in expressing himself in continuous prose. Two to three years should be spent on Part 1 which brings the student up to the level of the English Language paper of the Cambridge First Certificate in English examination. A further two years should be devoted to Part 2 which goes well beyond the requirements of the Cambridge Proficiency in English examination and should be found suitable for students doing advanced work in the writing of English as a foreign language.

L. G. A.

By the same author:

Sixty Steps to Précis
Poetry and Prose Appreciation for Overseas Students
Essay and Letter Writing
A First Book in Comprehension, Précis and Composition
The Carters of Greenwood (*Cineloops*)
Question and Answer: Graded Aural/Oral Exercises
For and Against
Reading and Writing English. *A First Year Programme for Children*
Guided Composition in English Language Teaching
Look, Listen and Learn! Sets 1–4 *An Integrated Course for Children*

LONGMAN STRUCTURAL READERS:
Detectives from Scotland Yard
Car Thieves
Worth A Fortune
April Fools' Day
Professor Boffin's Umbrella
Operation Mastermind

NEW CONCEPT ENGLISH:
First Things First *An Integrated Course for Beginners*
Practice and Progress *An Integrated Course for Pre-Intermediate Students*
Developing Skills *An Integrated Course for Intermediate Students*
Fluency in English *An Integrated Course for Advanced Students*

NEW CONCEPT ENGLISH *in two volume edition:*
First Things First Parts 1–2
Practice and Progress Parts 1–2

The sentence

Types

No matter how many ideas it may contain, a sentence must always express a complete thought. There are three types of sentence: *simple*, *compound*, and *complex*.

The *Simple Sentence* expresses one idea only. It has one subject and one predicate. Example:

The man (subject) knocked at the door (predicate).

The *Compound Sentence* contains more than one idea. In this type of sentence all the ideas expressed have an equal value. Example:

The man knocked at the door and waited for an answer.

The *Complex Sentence* contains one main idea (called the 'main clause') and one or more secondary ideas (called 'subordinate clauses'). Example:

As soon as he arrived at the house (subordinate clause) the man knocked at the door (main clause).

Joining sentences

The words which are used to combine sentences are called 'conjunctions'. In the exercises that follow you will practise some of the main ways in which different ideas can be joined to make complete sentences.

COMPOUND SENTENCES The main conjunctions used to form compound sentences are: *and, but, yet, so, both … and, either … or, neither … nor, not only … but.*

Complete the following sentences by choosing one of the two words given in brackets.

(a) (And, Both) my wife and I went out early yesterday.
(b) (Or, Either) we will have to wait for them, or we will have to leave a message.
(c) He neither took my advice (nor, or) his father's.

neither ... nor

Note that in the negative *both ... and* and *either ... or* become *neither ... nor*.

Exercise 1

Join the following pairs of sentences using the conjunctions given in brackets. When you have done so write similar sentences of your own.

1. He was in Italy last year. Now he has returned home. (*but*)
2. The talk on the radio was not amusing. It was not interesting. (*neither ... nor*)
3. He told me to leave. He told me never to call again. (*not only ... but*)
4. I have often invited him here. He has never come. (*yet*)
5. Hurry up. You will be late. (*or*)
6. The manager told him he must work hard. He must leave the firm. (*either ... or*)
7. She sent a present to my brother. She sent a present to me. (*both ... and*)
8. My mother lives abroad. My father lives abroad. (*both ... and*)
9. She finished her housework. She went out shopping. (*so/and*)
10. He does not eat too much. He does not drink too much. (*neither ... nor*)
11. He told me I could stay here. He told me I could go away. (*either ... or*)
12. I bought a new car last year. I am not satisfied with it. (*but*)
13. My wife will not go to the concert tonight. I will not to go the concert tonight. (*neither ... nor*)
14. He needs a new suit. He needs a new pair of shoes. (*not only ... but*)
15. I received your telegram. I received your letter. (*both ... and*)
16. We must score two more goals. We will lose the match. (*or*)
17. I forgot my umbrella. I had to return home. (*so/and*)
18. She bought very few things. She spent a lot of money. (*yet*)
19. He did not tell me the truth. I misunderstood him. (*either ... or*)
20. He learned how to read English. He learned how to write it. (*not only ... but*)

COMPLEX SENTENCES In the exercises that follow you will practise some of the main ways in which different ideas can be joined to make complex sentences.

Complete the following sentences by choosing one of the two words given in brackets.

(a) The gardener (who, which) works here is very good.

(b) The man (who, whom) you saw yesterday is my neighbour.
(c) He has received the money (which, who) I sent him.
(d) The men (who, whom) will be playing on Saturday all belong to our local club.

Exercise 2
Join the following pairs of sentences using the relative pronouns *who*, *whom*, *whose*, or *which* where necessary. When you have done so write similar sentences of your own.
1. Mr Jones bought a new house. He has furnished it beautifully.
2. I have been looking for this book everywhere. I have now found it.
3. There were a lot of people at the party. I had not met them before.
4. That is the man. I spoke to you about him last week.
5. The firemen went into the building. It was full of smoke.
6. I have a few relatives. They live in the country.
7. My sister's friend came to see me. Her parents died last year.
8. He worked at this factory all his life. This is the factory.
9. The vase was very valuable. My younger brother broke it.
10. A friend of mine will be coming tomorrow. I received a letter from him.
11. The man came to visit me. He has just arrived from the Far East.
12. There are several people here. I do not know their names.
13. Is he your friend? Did you go to the cinema with him yesterday?
14. He has sent me a number of letters. I haven't had time to answer them.
15. The elephants escaped from the circus. They have been caught.
16. The country house is very large. He lives in it during the summer.
17. The girl is our new secretary. You saw her a moment ago.
18. The actress lives next door. She is very famous.
19. The man had to pay a fine. His car was parked on the wrong side of the road.
20. He is a lazy student. I can never depend on him.

INDIRECT QUESTIONS Note that in sentences containing an indirect question the subject must always be placed before the verb.

Complete the following sentences by choosing one of the two phrases given in brackets.
(a) I cannot remember (where did I leave, where I left) my coat.
(b) He asked me (when would my brother, when my brother would) arrive.
(c) You did not tell me (how much this cost, how much did this cost.)

Exercise 3

Join the following pairs of sentences using the words *when, what, where, why,* and *how* where they are needed. Make any other changes necessary. When you have completed this exercise write similar sentences of your own.

1. Why did he refuse to see me? You must find out.
2. I must leave now. I have already told you the reason.
3. How did you find out my address? Please tell me.
4. This is the shop. She bought her new hat at this shop.
5. When did you last hear from him? Write and let me know.
6. He wanted me to do something for him. He did not tell me what it was.
7. What did he tell you? I would like to know.
8. How many letters did you write to him? You cannot remember.
9. Did he leave the firm? Ask him why.
10. When did you buy this picture? You must surely remember.
11. He asked me to meet him at a certain place. This is the place.
12. How did he recognize you? I can't understand it.
13. Where did he put the book I lent you? Please ask him.
14. What time does the train arrive? No one seems to know.
15. He was going somewhere. He would not tell me the place.

JOINING SENTENCES WITH CONJUNCTIONS (1) *as, since, because, now that.*

Complete the following sentences by choosing one of the two words or phrases given in brackets.
(a) We had to leave (why, because) it was so late.
(b) (Now that, So that) it has stopped raining, I shall not have to take an umbrella.

Exercise 4

Join the following pairs of sentences using the conjunctions given in brackets. When you have done so, write similar sentences of your own.

1. We did not expect you. You did not let us know you were coming. (*because*)
2. The shops have shut. We should go home. (*now that*)
3. You have not understood the question. I will repeat it. (*since*)
4. It is raining heavily. I will not go out. (*as*)
5. I did not tell him. I was afraid I would hurt his feelings. (*because*)
6. You had better not stay too long. I have a lot of work to do. (*as*)
7. We should go home. The sun has set. (*now that*)
8. He is sure to pass his examination. He has worked so hard. (*since*)
9. She has bought a car. It will be easy for her to get to work. (*now that*)
10. I did not go to the theatre. I could not get tickets. (*because*)

JOINING SENTENCES WITH CONJUNCTIONS (2) *so ... that, such ... that.*

Complete the following sentences by choosing one of the words or phrases given in brackets.
(a) He is (a so, such a) kind person that he is sure to help me.
(b) He was (such, so) pleased when he heard the news that he rang me up at once.
(c) It is (such a, a so) nice day, I cannot bear to stay indoors.

Exercise 5
Join the following pairs of sentences using *so ... that*, or *such ... that* where necessary. When you have done so, write similar sentences of your own.
  1. He was glad to see me. He asked me to stay the night.
  2. He was tired. He could not get up in the morning.
  3. I have many friends abroad. I cannot write to all of them.
  4. He is a good driver. I am surprised to hear he has had an accident.
  5. He is an interesting person. It is a pleasure to hear him talk.
  6. It is a good film. It would be a pity to miss it.
  7. She was very angry. She refused to see him.
  8. It is a beautiful evening. We should go for a walk.
  9. He is a shy person. He dislikes talking to strangers.
  10. We arrived early. We had to wait for over an hour.

JOINING SENTENCES WITH CONJUNCTIONS (3) *to, in order to, so as to,* (followed by an infinitive) and *so that, in order that,* (followed by may, might, can, could, shall, should, will and would).

Complete the following sentences by choosing one of the two words or phrases given in brackets.
(a) I went there (for to, to) see him.
(b) I ran quickly (in order to be not, in order not to be) late.
(c) The little boy hid behind the door (in order his aunt not to see him, in order that his aunt might not see him.)
(d) I'll come and fetch you from the station (so that you will not have to, in order you do not have to) walk as far as my house.

Exercise 6
Leaving out the verb 'to want' in each case, join the following pairs of sentences using the conjunctions given in brackets. When you have done so, write similar sentences of your own.
  1. He went to the library. He wanted to borrow a book (*to*)
  2. The student asked the teacher a question. He wanted to understand the exercise better. (*in order that*)
  3. The thief drove quickly out of town. He did not want the police to catch him. (*so that*)

4. I went to the theatre early. I wanted to get a seat. (*in order to*)
5. I rang up. I wanted to find out what time she would come. (*in order that*)
6. He went into the room quietly. He did not want to disturb his brother who was asleep. (*so as to*)
7. The conductor stopped the bus. A passenger wanted to get off. (*so that*)
8. I had to take a taxi this morning. I did not want to miss my train. (*in order that*)
9. She turned on the radio. She wanted her mother to hear the talk. (*so that*)
10. I went into the shop. I wanted to buy a watch. (*to*)
11. She went to the post-office. She wanted to post a letter. (*in order to*)
12. We left in a hurry. We did not want to be seen. (*so as to*)
13. I wrote to the travel agency. I wanted them to send me some information. (*in order that*)
14. The explorer wrote a book. He wanted everybody to learn about his journey. (*so that*)
15. Tell him I have left. I do not want him to trouble me again. (*so that*)

JOINING SENTENCES WITH CONJUNCTIONS (4) *although, even though, even if, however* (much, many, long etc.), *in spite of the fact that.*

Exercise 7
Leaving out the phrase *it does not matter if* where necessary, join the following pairs of sentences using the conjunctions given in brackets. When you have done so, write similar sentences of your own.
1. I wrote to him several times. I received no answer. (*although*)
2. He plays well. He is still not good enough for the football team. (*in spite of the fact that*)
3. We are determined to get there. It does not matter how far away it is. (*however*)
4. The journey takes too long. It does not matter if you go by plane. (*even if*)
5. I'm sure he won't come. It does not matter how long you wait. (*however*)
6. We are going on an excursion. The weather is bad. (*in spite of the fact that*)
7. He speaks French well. He has never been to France. (*even though*)
8. She was very busy. She was able to help me. (*although*)
9. I should not work for him if I were you. It does not matter if he offers you a big salary. (*even if*)
10. I still think the film is poor. It does not matter if so many people enjoyed it. (*even though*)

PARTICIPLES

Complete the following sentences by choosing one of the two words or phrases given in brackets.
(a) Seeing me coming (the man, the man he) ran towards me.
(b) (Turning the corner, When he turned the corner) the brick fell on his head.

Exercise 8

Join the following pairs of sentences using the participle construction. When you have done so, write similar sentences of your own.

1. He thought it was my birthday. He came to visit me.
2. I stopped at a corner. I asked a policeman the way.
3. She thought I was a friend of hers. She greeted me.
4. I was ill. I did not go to work yesterday.
5. They found the door shut. They had to climb through the window.
6. He decided not to wait any longer. He left the office.
7. The guard was killed. The prisoner escaped.
8. I saw the car coming. I did not cross the street.
9. He has been abroad for many years. He is now finding it difficult to settle down.
10. He was told to go. He left immediately.
11. He was not able to understand. He asked the teacher to explain.
12. I was afraid. I returned to my room.
13. He has been asked to leave. He went away at once.
14. She did not believe me. She went to see for herself.
15. I felt very tired. I went straight to bed.

Tenses

THE PAST AND PAST CONTINUOUS The past continuous tense is used often when one action is interrupted by another. Interruption is usually indicated by the words *when, as,* and *while.* Example:

I was writing a letter *when* the telephone rang.

Choose the correct form of the verbs given in brackets.

When I was young I often (went, was going) to my aunt's house. I (was playing, played) with my cousins from morning till night. Every day we (climbed, were climbing) the hills around the house and (were walking, walked) down to the sea. We occasionally (went, were going) swimming. At midday, we always (were returning, returned) home.

8 The Sentence

Exercise 9

Write the correct tense (past or past continuous) in place of the verbs in brackets in the following sentences. When you have done so, write similar sentences of your own.

1. Just as we (leave) the house, a friend (come) to see us.
2. When I (hear) the news, I (be) very upset.
3. I (write) a letter when my mother (call) me.
4. When I (be) a boy I often (go) fishing with my uncle.
5. While I (listen) to the news I (repair) my fountain-pen.
6. You (enjoy) Latin when you were at school?
7. I (see) him drive past as I (cross) the road.
8. My sister (work) as a typist before she got married.
9. The train (leave) just as we (arrive) at the station.
10. We (stand) on the corner when we (see) the accident.
11. While I (walk) to the market this morning I (meet) my next-door neighbour.
12. The lights (go) out last night while they (have) a party.
13. When we (be) on holiday we not (swim) because it was so cold.
14. She (play) the piano when the door-bell (ring).
15. The teacher (read) to us when a pupil suddenly (ask) a question.

SEQUENCE OF TENSES (1) When the main verb is in the past, all dependent or co-ordinate verbs must also be in the past.

Complete the following sentences by choosing one of the two words given in brackets.

(a) I went into the room next door and (tell, told) him not to make a noise.
(b) He told me he (will, would) finish early.
(c) He telephoned to say he (can, could) not come.
(d) My aunt said she (may, might) come tomorrow.

Exercise 10

Re-write the following sentences putting the verbs given in brackets in the correct tense. When you have done so, write similar sentences of your own paying special attention to the rule covering the sequence of tenses.

1. He rang me up several times but I (be) out every time he (call)
2. I thought it (rain) today.
3. He asked me if he (can) leave the room.
4. When he (ask) me I told him I never (be) here before.
5. I never thought I (see) you again.
6. He asked me if he (can) help me in any way.
7. I looked for my pen everywhere but (can) not find it.
8. As he (leave) the house he remembered he (forget) his coat.

9. ... you (remember) to turn off the lights when you left the room?
10. I opened the door and (find) him sitting at my desk.
11. I told him I (be) late because I (be) busy.
12. He asked me who my friend (be).
13. If this (cost) so much why did you buy it?
14. As she (not understand) what he said she (ask) him to repeat it.
15. He (hope) he might go to London but it (be) impossible.

SEQUENCE OF TENSES (2) After the words *when, before, until, as soon as, after*, and *unless* never use the future tense. These words should be followed by the simple present or the present perfect tenses.

Complete the following sentences by choosing one of the two words or phrases given in brackets.
(a) When I (shall see, see) him, I shall let you know.
(b) Before you (will come, come) home, please buy some fruit.
(c) He will get very angry as soon as he (will hear, hears) about this.

Exercise 11

Supply the correct form of the verbs in brackets. When you have done so, write similar sentences of your own.

1. Please let me know as soon as you (hear) from him.
2. I will not stay unless he (ask) me to.
3. She must remain here until she (finish) her work.
4. He will telephone me before he (leave).
5. We will tell him about it after he (arrive).
6. They will go on holiday as soon as the weather (improve).
7. When I (see) you I shall know more about it.
8. We shall wait here until the bus (arrive).
9. He hopes to go to a university when he (leave) school.
10. I promise I will speak to him as soon as he (come).

SEQUENCE OF TENSES (3) clauses with 'if'. The three basic forms are:
1. If he *invites* me I *shall go.*
2. If he *invited* me I *would* go.*
3. If he *had invited* me I *would have gone.*

Complete the following sentences by choosing one of the two words or phrases given in brackets.
(a) If I (would see, see) you next week, I will tell you what happened.
(b) I would not have come if I (knew, had known).

* Though the past of *shall* is *should*, in this type of sentence it is better to use the past of *will, would* as the word *should* often has the sense of *ought to* in English.

(c) If you wrote to me sometimes, you (would get, would have got) an answer.

Exercise 12

Supply the correct form of the verbs in brackets. When you have done so, write similar sentences of your own.

1. We shall stay at home if it (rain).
2. I would have been able to come if you (let) me know in time.
3. If I (be) in your position I would tell him exactly what happened.
4. If I (have) more money I would buy a car.
5. If the teacher (explain) more carefully they would have understood.
6. We will get there on time if the train (be) not late.
7. Did you ask him if he (want) to see me?
8. I could have finished yesterday if you (ring) me up.
9. This exercise would be less difficult if we (know) the rules.
10. Do you think it will be better if he (come) tomorrow?

Word order

Keep to the basic pattern: Subject/Verb/Object/Qualifying Phrases, as closely as possible. Though there are certain exceptions, a subject may only be separated from its verb by an adverb of frequency. (See below.)

Complete the following sentences by choosing one of the two words or phrases given in brackets.

(a) (Yesterday he, He yesterday) found (in his garden a coin, a coin in his garden.)
(b) I received (from my cousin an invitation to a party, an invitation to a party from my cousin.)

Exercise 13

Re-write the following sentences correctly. When you have done so write sentences of your own paying special attention to word order.

1. The captain ordered the men to throw into the sea the goods.
2. You will have to write twice this exercise.
3. I went out to buy a book which had written a friend of mine.
4. It is pleasant to spend sometimes an hour in a library.
5. The head-master gave to the boy some good advice.
6. On my way to the office happened something very funny.
7. They both again reached home.
8. Once used to live two detectives opposite our house.
9. I went into the room where was the thief hiding.
10. I used very often to visit in the country my uncle.

11. Suddenly arrived at the house relations whom he did not want to see.
12. I asked him how much had I to pay.
13. He last month drove into a tree his car.
14. Yesterday brought the post-man a letter which I had been expecting.
15. By the policeman the driver to move on was ordered.
16. The man at last after losing his way returned to the hotel.
17. From the shelf by someone the book was taken.
18. The teacher forgot our compositions to correct.
19. The friend from abroad whom I told you about has arrived.
20. I forgot on the letter I sent to write the address.

ADVERBS OF FREQUENCY Here are the most important of them: *generally, sometimes, often, frequently, rarely, seldom, ever, never, usually, occasionally, already, just* and *still*.

They may be placed:
(a) Before the main verb. (He often comes to see me.)
(b) After the first auxiliary in a component verb. (It might never have happened.)
(c) After the verb 'to be' – though they may be placed before to vary the emphasis. (He is usually late. Or: He usually is.)

Complete the following sentences by choosing one of the two words or phrases given in brackets.
(a) He (often comes, comes often) to see me.
(b) If you had been careful this (never might, might never) have happened.
(c) He (has rarely, rarely has) taken much trouble with his work.
(d) He (is already, already is) here.

Exercise 14
Put the adverbs given in brackets in their correct place in each of these sentences.
1. He has mentioned the subject. (*never*)
2. It is raining hard. (*still*)
3. We go to this part of the town. (*seldom*)
4. He is ill. (*often*)
5. These adverbs go before the main verb. (*generally*)
6. He has invited me to his house. (*sometimes*)
7. She would have told you a thing like that. (*never*)
8. You can trust him. (*always*)
9. He goes out of the house. (*rarely*)
10. You can be certain that he will succeed. (*never*)

Common mistakes

Exercise 15

Re-write the following sentences in correct English.

1. Your hands are not very clear.
2. At last the ship it managed to rich the harbour.
3. Nobody said nothing for what had happened.
4. He was enjoyied his travel very much.
5. The sun was shinning at the sea.
6. We went for a walk with our car.
7. The storm cause a very big damage.
8. He did not leave me to go.
9. I tryed to find the luggages who I had left at the platform.
10. We did not have a moment to loose.
11. The afternoon I went for a walk with a friend of me.
12. For my good luck he told me the hole story.
13. We saw the boat to sink and run for help.
14. I did not afraid when I herd it.
15. People use to say that it was not a so easy thing to travel with a plane.
16. I am enough comfortable he told.
17. Sometimes when it happens the sea to be rough we do not go for baths.
18. The teacher, he explained us our mistakes as usually.
19. He went at school early this morning without to eat any breakfast.
20. He is the friend of her's.
21. What shall I do with all these money?
22. The bad was that we could not to go home.
23. He said us much stories.
24. He is bigger than me one year.
25. They wanted to make us a surprise.
26. This tree has grown up a lot.
27. I have been hear since five years.
28. The science has improved our lifes.
29. They hanged the picture from the wall.
30. As soon as I will return at home I will go to the bed.
31. I am thinking to go to England next year.
32. He threw to the dog a stone.
33. They did not obey to the teacher when he told them to be quite.
34. Last night were many thunders and lightnings.
35. He has not succeed to pass his examination.
36. We were told to work very hardly.
37. They asked each to the other for help.

38. Everybody in the church were quiet.
39. He fell down of his chair.
40. We stoped out of the hotel to wait our friend.
41. I saw a dream yesterday in the night.
42. In the dark room I fell on the wardrobe.
43. Something prevented it to open.
44. The table's leg is broken.
45. He said me the police has catched the thief.
46. It likes me to travel with a ship.
47. Except what I told you, you must to remember to write clearly.
48. We reached to the house early and knocked the door.
49. It seemed going to rain.
50. I told to her to do'nt trouble me.
51. We run over the bridge but still we lost the train.
52. We went to bed early because the other day we were going to do an excursion.
53. Many people is hear.
54. I was afraid what would happened.
55. I passed wonderful the holidays.
56. By this way you will learn how to swim.
57. He is the man who he lost his case.
58. For my surprise the lesson had began.
59. I had ten days to see you.
60. When he was ill he was laying in bed for weeks.
61. This morning we heared a terrible new.
62. I opened the radio for to hear the speach.
63. His hairs are turning grey.
64. He told me he will leave and so he did.
65. Do not make noise.
66. He went at the garden to cut some woods.
67. A passenger in the street walked passed my house.
68. Entering into the room he opened the light.
69. A day we went a walk.
70. The woman wich lives next door says this kind of things.
71. We do not wait the train to arrive on time.
72. This team won them before a week.
73. The whole class was too shocked when they heard the news.
74. The man controlled my passport.
75. They stole our house last weak.
76. My car is the same with your.
77. I had breakfast. After I went for shopping.
78. He raised from the chair because he was very hurry.
79. In the way to the station I met my friend.

80. I left from my house early today morning.
81. Do not say to them anything.
82. I felt asleep on the train.
83. I have many works to do.
84. My worse enemy is the laziness.
85. He has very few cloths and does not dress good.
86. He was dressed with a new costume.
87. We were discussing about the political position.
88. I could not opened the garden's gate.
89. That lady is our new typewriter.
90. From the very begining I was sure nothing wrong happened.
91. The man put fire to the rubbish.
92. It was brocken to peaces.
93. The enemys attacked against us.
94. We laughted allowed.
95. The buss ran fastly in order that the children arrived quickly to the school.
96. He borrowed me some money.
97. He was hearing the results from the radio.
98. In the contrary of my brother I work hardly.
99. This informations are not truth.
100. Do not do so many mistakes!

The paragraph narrative and descriptive

Building up your paragraph

Instructions

1. Choose a title which interests you.
2. Think carefully about what you are going to say before writing.
3. Always indent the first sentence of your paragraph.
4. Try to make your story or description interesting from the very first sentence.
5. The first sentence should give the reader some idea of what the paragraph is about.
6. Write short, complete sentences.
7. Keep to the subject.
8. Take great care to connect your sentences so that your work reads smoothly. Words like 'but', 'since', 'although', 'after', 'afterwards', 'meanwhile' etc. will enable you to do this.
9. Save the most interesting part until the end or near the end.
10. Work neatly. Make sure your writing is clear, your spelling and punctuation correct and that there are margins to the left and right of your work.
11. Abbreviations like 'don't', 'haven't', 'wouldn't' etc. are not normally used in written English. Write out the words in full: 'do not', 'have not', 'would not' etc.
12. *Never on any account* write your paragraph in your mother-tongue and then attempt to translate it into English.
13. Avoid using a dictionary. Never use words that are entirely new to you.
14. When you have finished, read your work through and try to correct mistakes you may have made in grammar.

Narrative

In narrative compositions you are required to tell a story or write about an event. Always tell things in the order in which they happened. Some of your stories may be written in dialogue if you wish, but take great care to punctuate direct speech correctly. Do not use dashes in place of inverted commas, or employ quotation marks which are not normally used in English. It is generally preferable to keep to the past tense.

Read carefully the paragraph that follows.

Follow that Bus!

I jumped off the bus before it stopped and began walking down the street. As I had arrived early, I decided to look at the shop windows before going home. The idea made me quite happy, but at the same time I had the unpleasant feeling that I had forgotten something. I stopped in the middle of the pavement and began searching my pockets. All of a sudden I remembered that I was without my briefcase! I had left it on the bus and it was full of important papers. The thought was enough to make me start running down the street, though, by now, the bus was out of sight.

Answer these questions:

1. What do we learn in the first sentence and how is this related to the rest of the story?
2. What words and phrases are used to connect the sentences to each other?
3. What is the main idea in the story and in which sentence is it to be found?
4. How is each sentence in the paragraph related to this main idea?
5. Are things told in the order in which they happened? What is the sequence of events?

Exercises

Instructions

Write one-paragraph stories using each of the sentences given below. The length should be about 100 words; do not include the sentence or sentences given in the total number of words.

You should spend about 25 minutes on each paragraph. The best way to divide your time is as follows: thinking your story through: about 5 minutes; writing: about 15 minutes; re-reading: about 5 minutes. Give each story a title.

Numbers 1–10 should form the first sentences of your paragraphs; numbers 11–20 the last; in numbers 21–30 you have been given the first and last and should supply those which come between.

First Sentences

1. I tore the letter open impatiently.
2. As soon as he heard the clock strike three, he knew it was too late.
3. No matter what we did, the car simply refused to start.
4. I have never seen anyone climb over a wall so quickly.

5. 'And what is behind this little door?' asked the lady in a strange voice.
6. For the first time since our arrival we realized that the villagers were unfriendly and suspicious.
7. I could hardly believe my eyes when I saw a piano in the middle of the lawn.
8. Nobody ever dared to argue with father.
9. The next morning I decided to ask the boss to raise my salary.
10. 'The person most likely to know,' thought Gregg as he walked down the street, 'would be the barber.'

Last Sentences

11. 'Now you can open your eyes,' they said.
12. We swam back to the other side as quickly as we could.
13. The woman had mistaken me for a thief!
14. In spite of our efforts, we still had not managed to wake him up.
15. This time, however, he reached out too far and lost his balance.
16. The angry farmer had set the dog free and it was running towards them.
17. Then we suddenly realized that the man was going to jump off the roof.
18. There was no one in the room and a cigarette was burning away in the ash-tray.
19. I saw the precious piece of paper floating away down the river.
20. I had forgotten that banks usually shut so early.

First and Last Sentences

21. (a) 'I don't like this hat either,' said the lady.
    (b) The floor was covered with hats.
22. (a) I hastily got out of the bath to answer the telephone.
    (b) 'I said you've got the wrong number!' I repeated angrily.
23. (a) 'It's your last chance,' said a voice.
    (b) Someone had forgotten to turn the radio off.
24. (a) 'But I haven't any money,' I said to the waiter.
    (b) I spent half the night washing dishes.
25. (a) I reached the station just as the train was leaving.
    (b) 'There won't be another one till tomorrow morning,' said the porter.
26. (a) For Paul, piano lessons were particularly painful.
    (b) 'Now take it again from the beginning!' said Miss Henke sharply.

27. (a) 'Where are we?' asked John.
    (b) 'We're on the wrong bus,' answered his sister.
28. (a) He took a step backwards and there was a loud crash.
    (b) To his horror, he saw it was the expensive vase everyone had been talking about.
29. (a) The man hit the policeman so hard that he fell down.
    (b) Then I understood that they were making a film!
30. (a) 'I've won a prize in the lottery!' shouted father.
    (b) You can imagine his disappointment when he found out that he had made a mistake.

Descriptive

In descriptive compositions you are generally required to describe people, objects, or scenes. Your description may take the form of a personal impression or may be purely imaginary. Whatever the case, try to include interesting details.

Read carefully the paragraph that follows.

Under the Sea

The diver could just see a dark mass near the rocks. He swam nearer and after turning on his torch, he was able to make out the remains of an old ship. It was covered with mud and shells. Fish swam through a great hole in its side. The diver went through the hole and came to what had once been the engine-room. In the torchlight it looked empty and ghostly. Sea-weeds seemed to grow out of the ship's engines so that they took strange shapes. As he looked round him, the diver found it hard to believe that men had once worked there.

Answer these questions:

1. What do we learn from the first sentence and how is it related to what follows?
2. What words and phrases are used to connect the sentences to each other?
3. Would you say that this description is a personal impression or purely imaginary? Why?
4. What is the writer setting out to describe?
5. How is each sentence related to the main idea?
6. What details in the description seem to you especially interesting? Why?

Exercises

Instructions

Write one-paragraph descriptions using each of the sentences given below. The length should be about 100 words; do not include the sentence or sentences given in the total number of words.

You should spend about 25 minutes on each paragraph. The best way to divide your time is as follows: thinking out your description: about 5 minutes; writing: about 15 minutes; re-reading: about 5 minutes. Give each description a title.

Numbers 1–10 should form the first sentences of your paragraphs; numbers 11–20 the last; in numbers 21–30 you have been given the first and last and should supply those which come between.

First Sentences

1. At night the main street of the town is brilliantly lit.
2. Everyone turned round to look at the man who had entered the restaurant.
3. The bus was so crowded I could hardly breathe.
4. I lay in bed warm and comfortable listening to the rain beating against the windows.
5. The house next door to ours is very large.
6. The climb to the top of the tower had been well worth the effort.
7. My first experience of life was my grandmother's death.
8. A huge crowd had collected to look at the hole in the road.
9. The room was beautifully furnished.
10. The flood-water reached its highest point next day.

Last Sentences

11. We were all relieved to hear that aunt Beatrice had decided to leave.
12. The ship had now become a dot on the horizon.
13. It was the best game I had ever seen.
14. We learnt later that the zebra had escaped from the circus.
15. Just missing the tree-tops, the plane landed in the field.
16. We prepared to spend yet another night in the desert.
17. Just at this point I woke up.
18. From where I stood, I could just see a small white house at the bottom of the valley.
19. The snow had now begun to melt.
20. He was certainly the strangest man I have ever met.

First and Last Sentences

21. (a) The voice was familiar but I could not recognize the face.
    (b) His disguise was perfect.

22. (a) The drunk was leaning against a lamp-post talking to himself.
    (b) Just as I came near he suddenly asked me what day it was.
23. (a) The landlady led me up the stairs to see the room.
    (b) I left so quickly I did not even say good-bye.
24. (a) It had not rained for six weeks.
    (b) Now dark storm clouds gathered in the sky.
25. (a) The water in the lake had frozen hard.
    (b) Even children of two were trying to skate.
26. (a) I shall never forget my old head-master.
    (b) After all these years he remembers every one of his old pupils.
27. (a) At the first stroke of twelve, the figures on the clock began moving.
    (b) Now the figures would remain still for another twelve hours.
28. (a) It was the best window display I had ever seen.
    (b) This beautiful scene had been created with just a few objects.
29. (a) My desk was in a terrible mess.
    (b) I wondered how long it would remain tidy.
30. (a) A bird flew down from the tree and rested on the fence.
    (b) Sensing danger, the bird flew away just as the cat was ready to spring.

The essay narrative and descriptive

Building up your essay

Instructions

1. INTEREST Writing an essay is not simply a matter of getting the required number of words down on paper. You must do all you can to make your essays *interesting* so that they will hold the reader's attention to the very end. To achieve this it is not necessary to go to absurd lengths to be original. All you need do is to include incidents and details which are drawn from everyday life or which you have imagined.

The most unpromising subject can be turned into an exciting essay. Let us suppose that you have to write about 'A Day at the Seaside'. This may seem to you a typically 'dull' topic. If all you have to say in the 300 or so words at your disposal is that you went to the beach, had a swim, had something to eat, and then went home, you will have written a typically dull composition. An essay can be as dull or as interesting as you care to make it. Here are a few details which could be included in this particular topic: the colourful scene on the beach: sun-shades, tents, bathing-costumes; sun – or rain; sunbathing; children building sand-castles – looking for shells; games on the beach; people afraid to take the first plunge; people in difficulties in the sea; learning to swim; the pleasure of swimming; diving; water-skiing; coming out of the water; hot sand; sand in your hair, your clothes; people burying themselves in sand; a picnic on the beach; a restaurant; a fun-fair; the journey home: hot, tired, happy, still thinking of the sea. Once you have found something definite to say, your essay will be interesting to read.

2. UNITY Just as it is important to connect your sentences *within* a paragraph, you should make sure that your paragraphs lead on naturally to each other. Answer the question closely. Do not repeat yourself. Make sure that every paragraph adds something new to the essay.

3. BALANCE AND PROPORTION Keep a sense of proportion. The length of a paragraph will depend on what you have to say; however do not let yourself be carried away by fascinating but unimportant details. If, for instance, in the subject given above, you were to spend a whole page describing how you got to the seaside and then one or two paragraphs more to say what you did there, your essay would be *unbalanced*. Never attempt to write an essay in a single paragraph.

4. PERSONAL STATEMENTS Do not address the teacher or make comments on the topic like, 'I do not like this subject and do not know how to begin' or, '... and now it is time for me to finish my essay' etc.

5. TEST FOR QUALITY If in your effort to reach the word-limit you find yourself counting the number of words you have used every time you add another sentence to the essay, it is a sure sign that there is something basically wrong with your treatment of the subject. If you are so bored with your own writing that you have to keep counting the number of words to find out if you are nearing the end, it is more than likely that your teacher will be equally bored when he has to read what you have written. If your essay gave you pleasure to write, it is quite probable that it will be enjoyable to read. This is a good – but not always reliable – test for quality.

6. RE-READING It is absolutely necessary to read your work through when you have finished writing. While doing so, keep a sharp look out for grammatical mistakes – especially those connected with word order or the sequence of tenses. Try to develop the habit of not repeating a mistake once it has been pointed out to you.

7. TITLES After you have finished your essay choose a good short title. Make sure that it has to do with the subject, but it should not give the reader *too* much information.

Narrative

PLANNING When telling a story, it is always best to relate events in the order in which they happened. Your first paragraph should set the scene. The most exciting part of your story should come at the end. In this way you will keep the reader in suspense. Do not spoil your story by 'throwing away' the most interesting part of it in the first sentence or paragraph.

The general outline for stories should be as follows:

Before the event
The event
After the event

Before working on your plan try to decide what the main event will be so that you can build your story round it. It is not always necessary to make out a full, detailed plan. But it is wise to note a few ideas under each heading so that you have a fairly clear picture of what you are going to say before you begin writing. Remember that a plan is only a *guide*. It is always possible to ignore your original scheme if a more interesting way of developing your story suddenly occurs to you after you have begun writing. Cross out your plan neatly with a single line when you have completed it so that it is possible for your teacher to refer to it if necessary.

Examine carefully the plan below, then read the essay that follows.

TITLE   The Stranger on the Bridge.
MAIN EVENT Late at night a man climbs over a wall surrounding a big house.

PLAN

Before the event
1. Midnight: bridge – cold – dark.
2. Frank on bridge. Someone approaching. Effect on him.
3. Steps come nearer. Frank turns to look.
4. Pretends to stop – sees stranger: description.
The event
5. Conversation: man wants information.
6. Frank suspicious. Why? Follows. Outside house: lights, man over wall.
After the event
7. Frank now sure – telephone-box.

The Stranger on the Bridge

The big Town Hall clock was striking midnight when Frank began to cross the bridge. The night air was cold and damp. A low mist hung over the river and the street-lamps gave little light.

Frank was anxious to get home and his footsteps rang loudly on the pavement. When he reached the middle of the bridge he thought he could hear someone approaching behind him. He looked back but could see no one. However, the sound continued and Frank began walking more quickly. Then he slowed down again, ashamed of himself for acting so foolishly. There was nothing to fear in a town as quiet as this.

The short, quick steps grew louder until they seemed very near. Frank found it impossible not to turn round. As he did so, he caught sight of a figure coming towards him.

After reaching the other side of the bridge, Frank stopped and pretended to look down at the water. From the corner of his eye he could now make out the form of a man dressed in a large overcoat. A hat was pulled down over his eyes and very little of his face could be seen.

As the man came near, Frank turned towards him and said something about the weather in an effort to be friendly. The man did not answer but asked gruffly where Oakfield House was. Frank pointed to a big house in the distance and the stranger continued his way.

The inquiry made Frank suspicious because he knew that the in-habitants of Oakfield House were very wealthy. Almost without realizing what he was doing, he began following the stranger quietly. The man was soon outside the house and Frank saw him look up at the windows. A light was still on and the man waited until it went out. When about half an hour had passed, Frank saw him climb noiselessly over the wall and heard him drop on to the ground at the other side.

Now Frank's worst suspicions were confirmed. He walked quickly and silently across the street towards a telephone-box on the corner.

Answer these questions:

1. What relationship is there between the plan and the story?
2. Pick out as many details as you can which you think have been in-cluded to make the story interesting.
3. What is the function of the first paragraph in the story?
4. Where is the most exciting part of the story to be found?
5. Show how the paragraphs lead on naturally to one another. How has this been done?
6. How does the idea of the bridge give the story its unity?
7. Do you consider the story to be well-balanced? Give reasons for your answer.
8. How suitable is the title?

Exercises

Instructions

Write stories using each of the paragraphs given below. The length should be between 250 and 350 words; do not include the paragraph or paragraphs given in the total number of words.

You should spend about an hour and a quarter on each story. The best way to divide your time is as follows: plan: 10–15 minutes; writing: 45–50 minutes; re-reading: 10–15 minutes. Give each story a title.

Numbers 1–10 should form the first paragraphs of your stories; numbers 11–20 the last; in numbers 21–30 you have been given the first and last and should supply those which come between.

First Paragraphs

1. Mr Soames woke up with a start and was surprised to find the gallery so quiet and almost dark. Just in front of him on the wall there was a forgotten painting by some Old Master. As he looked at it, he suddenly remembered where he was. The dreadful realization came over him all at once: he had been shut up in the museum!

2. The man opposite me in the train was pretending to read a newspaper. Every time I looked up, I found that he was looking at me over the top of the paper. I pretended not to notice, but the man's strange expression made me feel nervous. In the end, I could not bear it any longer, so I got up and went into the corridor.

3. The restaurant did not seem very inviting. The windows looked as if they had not been cleaned for months. In one of them there was a notice saying 'Cook Wanted'. The words had been clumsily printed on a dirty piece of paper. A little man in a coat much too big for him stood looking at it for several minutes. At last he seemed to make up his mind and opened the door.

4. Just as we tried to overtake the bus, a huge five-ton lorry suddenly turned out of a side-street, cutting in front of us. We were obliged to crawl along slowly at twenty miles an hour. As we gazed at the back of the lorry, we wondered whether we would ever be able to get to the harbour in time.

5. I shall never forget the first time I tried to ride a bicycle. It was a very big one, I remember, far too big for me. But I wanted to learn very much and nothing could stop me. I wheeled it up to the top of a hill and, with the help of a friend, got on. In a short time I was moving slowly down the hill with my hands on the brakes.

6. Mrs Wilkinson got a shock when she entered the room. Grouped in a circle round two small tables were a number of unshaven, poorly-dressed men. They were playing cards and they stopped talking the moment she appeared. As she stood there, one of the men made a sign to the others and then got up and walked towards her.

7. It was some time before I realized that I had been turned into a cat. The first thing I noticed was that I was sitting on the floor instead of on the chair. My clothes were in a heap by the chair as if I had just stepped out of them. On the small table the glass was still half-full of the black, bitter liquid I had drunk. I tried to stand up on two feet and succeeded only in standing on four. Then I began to walk with a curious springy motion. Suddenly the door opened and Julia came in. I tried to say 'Julia' and heard myself let out a discordant 'miaow'!

8. The small party of men came to a halt at the top of the hill at a signal from their leader. They first threw down their rifles, then, unbuckling their heavy ammunition belts, they let them slide to their feet. All the men except the leader dropped wearily to the ground and lay there motionless. The leader was a tall bearded man who wore a curious khaki-coloured peak cap. As he stood there, he kept scanning the countryside from left to right through field-glasses, watching for any sign of movement.

9. Suddenly I felt someone pushing the wardrobe from behind. It went

over with a loud crash – and I went over with it. I could not help screaming and I immediately heard footsteps hurrying up the stairs. They had found out where I was! As I lay there, I tried to think of what I was going to say to explain why I had hidden in the wardrobe in the first place.

10. Ten short quick steps brought him to the other side of the room. There was a sound of breaking glass. In a moment he had jumped out of the window and was halfway across the garden before anyone could stop him.

Last Paragraphs

11. The tree was just touching the other side of the bank. It was not a very safe bridge, but we went across one by one. As the last man reached the bank, the trunk slid down the side and fell heavily into the water. The river swiftly carried away the 'bridge' that had saved us and we watched it till it was out of sight.

13. I was so glad when I heard a key in the front door. Looking after the baby had been very hard work – much harder than I had expected.

13. A great pile of metal lay on the floor – all that was left of the terrible robot. Its electric eyes shone brightly as if it was still alive even after having been blown to pieces. But we knew that it would never trouble us again.

14. 'You are mistaken, madam,' said the old gentleman rather stiffly. 'You see, my name is Willis not Wells.'

'Oh, dear!' exclaimed the lady.

15. The tail of the plane was in flames and the pilot knew he would not be able to land safely. There was another burst just behind him. This time he pressed a button, pulled the rip cord and suddenly found himself sailing through space. Soon the parachute billowed out and as he swung in mid-air, he saw his plane crash into the field below where it seemed to explode like a bomb.

16. Just then the boss came in. I smiled up at him and began explaining what I had been doing. But I hardly had time to utter a word. 'You're fired!' he shouted as soon as he saw me. Then he went out quickly slamming the door behind him.

17. 'I'm afraid I haven't heard a thing,' replied the old lady loudly. 'I've been trying to tell you so for the last half-hour but you just wouldn't listen: I'm deaf!'

18. At dawn the train stopped at a small country station and I was able to buy a sandwich and a cup of coffee. We had at last got over the border and I knew that in another two hours our long and uncomfortable journey would be over.

19. Mr Trench opened the front door quickly and was surprised to find

a number of letters on the floor in the hall. He picked them up hurriedly and went through them one by one. Tears came into his eyes when he saw a thin yellow envelope. He realized with dismay that his telegram had not been received.

20. The members of the search-party sat down to rest in a small clearing in the wood. After two sleepless nights they had at last found the missing boy. He was sleeping peacefully under a tree only half a mile away from his home.

First and Last Paragraphs

21. (a) It is hard for people who live under blue skies to imagine what a heavy city fog is like. It is something quite different from the clear mist on a mountain and may come down without warning and cover a whole town.

   (b) I climbed the steps of every entrance until I came to my own. Even when I had opened the door, I was not sure that it was the right house or even the right street!

22. (a) It had been a hard day's climb. The two climbers had reached a small lake and they decided to spend the night ther   It was getting dark and David said he would gather sticks to light a fire. Robert said he would go to the top of the mountain and return in about an hour.

   (b) The light of a fire just ahead showed Robert that he was not far from the camp. He was very grateful to David for having gathered sticks and lit a fire. Otherwise he would have been completely lost.

23. (a) At the widest part of the river the two men decided to row to the bank and have a rest. They had a good lunch in the shade of the trees. Now the afternoon sun made them feel sleepy. They lay back in the boat and soon they were fast asleep.

   (b) They climbed on to the slippery rock with difficulty. From there they could see their boat further down the river. It was caught between a tree-trunk and some stones. The water rushed past them, and as they looked at their boat, they wondered how they would ever reach it.

24. (a) 'Good-morning, madam,' said the salesman, raising his hat. 'I'm from the "Nusweep Cleaner Company". I'm sure you will be interested in this new carpet sweeper. It is the very latest model. May I come in and show you how it works? You are, of course, under no obligation to buy it.'

   (b) 'All I know, young man,' said Mrs Bright angrily as she handed the salesman a broom, 'is that you are not leaving this house till you have cleaned my carpet and dusted my furniture!'

25. (a) When the ship began to roll, I left the smoke-filled bar and

decided to sit on deck. A storm at sea is something I enjoy immensely – perhaps because I have never been seasick. I love watching the waves crashing against the sides of the boat, knowing that I am in the heart of a storm and yet safe on board.

(b) The noise of the ship's engines ceased and members of the crew were quickly lowering a life-boat. By now, the man was about a hundred yards away, clinging to the life-jacket and waving to the crew. The life-boat touched the water and the crew made ready to rescue the man who was vainly trying to swim towards them.

26. (a) When we moved into our new house Betty and I decided to decorate it ourselves. I had never held a paint-brush in my life, but I was quite sure it would be easy. We bought paint and brushes and were soon ready to start.

(b) 'The first thing I shall do tomorrow morning,' said Betty, 'will be to ring up a decorator to come and do the job properly!' I could not have agreed more!

27. (a) The day father decided to fell the great oak-tree in our garden, the whole family gathered round to watch. He had long declared that he was against trees and especially the ones round the house which, he said, made the place damp and gloomy. Mother did her best to dissuade him saying that he would bring the whole building down on our heads and kill us all.

(b) The tree leaned over for a moment, then, with a great grinding noise, wrenched itself free from the stump and crashed to the ground. Mother shut her eyes at this moment. When she opened them again, she seemed surprised to find the tree had fallen just where father had planned and that the house was still standing.

28. (a) It was getting quite late and I knew that if I did not find a hotel soon I would have to sleep on a park-bench or in a police-station. I had been searching in vain for three hours and was feeling so hungry that I decided to go into the little restaurant I had passed some moments before. The drawn curtains, the dim light and loud sound of music coming from inside did not make the place very attractive, but I had no choice and went in.

(b) I tried to go off to sleep but could not. There was a strange sound coming from the room next door and the noisy music from downstairs was unbearable. I could hear people walking and talking in the corridor outside and had the feeling that something odd was going on. In the end I got up, turned on the light and went to the door. I tried to open it and found that it had been locked – from outside!

29. (a) As the goods train moved out of the small country railway-station, two figures darted from behind some bushes and leapt on to the moving wagons. They were quite unobserved as it was well after mid-

night and there were few people about. The men had escaped from a prison-camp three days earlier and had been trying to reach the frontiers of a neutral country which they had calculated must be about ninety miles distant.

(b) An astonished guard saw two men lying still among empty tins and paper wrappings. Both men resigned themselves to their fate and slowly raised their hands. The guard laughed loudly when he saw this. There was nothing to fear, he told them: they were on neutral ground!

30. (a) The whole building was in flames. In the street below, a large crowd looked up anxiously at the four men on the roof. The flames were getting higher and higher and at any moment part of the building might fall down. The fire-brigade had arrived but the building was so high that jumping would mean certain death.

(b) Just as the last of the four men had climbed up the ladder which was hanging from the helicopter, there was a loud noise. The crowd saw the building sway for a moment. Then it crashed down into the flames.

Descriptive

PLANNING In many ways it is easier to plan a story since the events you relate are in chronological order and therefore your essay has a natural beginning, middle, and end. In descriptive essays, however, there is no underlying 'story' to hold your composition together so it is necessary to think of a *central idea* to which everything you describe can be related. If, for instance, the subject is 'A Market' you will find it much easier to write if you can think of an interesting approach to the question first. In this case, the central idea could be the great variety of things for sale, or you could concentrate mainly on the different types of people selling goods and buying them. Once you have struck on a central idea you immediately have something definite to write about.

There is also another important difference between narrative and description. In descriptive writing, there is no single event which will keep the reader in suspense as there is in a story. Whether or not your essay will be exciting to read will depend entirely on the interesting details you include. In your first paragraph you should consider the subject in general and deal with details in the paragraphs that follow. Your description may take the form of a personal impression or may be purely imaginary.

The general outline for descriptive essays should be as follows:

    Introduction

    Development

    Conclusion

It is absolutely necessary to make out a plan noting a few ideas under each heading. In this way you will avoid repeating yourself. As in

narrative essays, however, the plan is only a guide and you may depart
from it if in the course of writing you think of a more interesting way of
dealing with the subject. Cross out your plan neatly with a single line
when you have completed it so that it is possible for your teacher to refer
to it if necessary.

Examine carefully the plan below, then read the essay that follows.

TITLE   A Walk on Sunday Morning
CENTRAL IDEA A day spent in the city can be quite as interesting as one
               in the country.

PLAN

Introduction
1. Decision to spend day in city: square – gardens. First impressions.
Development
2. Arrival at square: people – pigeons – statue. Incident: boy and
   pigeons.
3. Leave square. Public Gardens: different atmosphere.
4. Pond most interesting. Various boats.
5. Rest. Join crowd – man – model of ship.
Conclusion
6. Midday. Leave for home. Surprise that city could be so pleasant.

A Walk on Sunday Morning

Though I usually go on excursions to the country during the week-end, I
had decided to spend the whole of Sunday in the city for a change and to
visit the central square and public gardens. It was so early when I left
home that the streets were deserted. Without the usual crowds and
traffic, everything was strangely quiet.

When, at last, I arrived at the square I was surprised to find so many
people there. Some were feeding pigeons and others were sitting
peacefully at the foot of a tall statue. I went and sat with them so as to
get a better view. What amused me most was a little boy who was trying
to make pigeons fly up to his shoulder. He was holding some bird-seed in
his hand and whenever a pigeon landed on his arm, he laughed so much
that he frightened the bird away.

Some time later I made my way to the public gardens. Here there was
an entirely different atmosphere. The sun was now bright and warm
and the air was filled with gay laughter.

The pond interested me more than anything else for many people had
come to sail model boats. There were little yachts with bright red sails,
motor boats and wonderful sailing ships. They moved gracefully across

the water carried by the wind while their owners waited for them to reach the other side.

After resting for a time under a tree, I went and joined a number of people who had gathered round a man with a big model of a famous sailing ship called 'The Cutty Sark'. It was perfectly made and I gazed at it with admiration as its owner placed it in the water where it sailed majestically among the ducks and swans.

At midday, I left the gardens and slowly began walking home. I was not at all sorry that I had not gone to the country for the week-end. There had been much more to see in the city on a Sunday morning than I could ever have imagined.

Answer these questions:

1. What is the relationship between the plan and the essay?
2. Pick out details which make the description interesting.
3. In what way does the first paragraph introduce the description? How is it related to the last paragraph?
4. Show how the paragraphs lead on naturally to one another. How has this been done?
5. How does the writer indicate (a) that he moves from place to place (b) that time has passed?
6. In what way does the central idea give the essay its unity?
7. Do you consider that the description is well-balanced? Give reasons for your answer.
8. How suitable is the title?

Exercises

Instructions

Write descriptive essays using each of the paragraphs given below. The length should be between 250 and 350 words; do not include the paragraph or paragraphs given in the total number of words.

You should spend about an hour and a quarter on each essay. The best way to divide your time is as follows: plan: 10–15 minutes; writing: 45–50 minutes; re-reading: 10–15 minutes. Give each essay a title.

Numbers 1–10 should form the first paragraphs of your essays; numbers 11–20 the last; in numbers 21–30 you have been given the first and last and should supply those that come between.

First Paragraphs

1. It is always pleasant to look through an old photograph album. Hundreds of people are gathered there together: grandparents, parents, uncles, aunts, cousins, and friends. For a short time, it is possible to see them all again in some of the happiest moments of their lives.

2. Near our house there is an old tunnel through which runs a disused and very rusty railway line. One day, armed with a powerful torch, I decided to walk through it to see where it led to.

3. Last year preparations for Christmas began even earlier than usual. The shops had begun displaying Christmas presents almost two months before. As the big day drew nearer, the gay decorations in the streets and the huge number of people out shopping made our town almost unrecognizable.

4. He was a short well-built man with an ugly face and an equally ugly dog. If anyone ever passed his house, the dog would rush to the gate barking furiously. This was the sort of thing that pleased him most. At such moments his face would appear at the window and he would laugh loudly. He seemed to enjoy frightening people and it was this that made everyone dislike him so much.

5. When I joined the queue at the bus-stop everybody was complaining that they had been standing in the rain for twenty minutes and there was still no sign of a bus. I buttoned up my overcoat and put my hands into my pockets to keep warm. Since all these people had been waiting for so long I was sure a bus would appear soon.

6. I liked the house from the moment I saw it. After months of searching, I was delighted to find such a gay little cottage. Climbing rose-bushes had completely covered the front and there was a beautiful, well-kept garden all round.

7. From far away, the old fortress looked a complete ruin. Its grey ancient walls had tumbled down in places and the tall tower with its tiny windows looked as though it would fall at any moment – which was un-likely because it had stood for centuries. The original building had been put up in Roman times, but the tower and the greater part of what remained had been built in the Middle Ages. A deep moat had been dug round the fortress, though the old draw-bridge had long ago fallen to pieces. In its place a small wooden bridge had been built mainly for the benefit of tourists.

8. Few things can be more unpleasant than having to cancel an excursion because of the weather. Your first glimpse of the morning you hoped would be so fine is not very encouraging. By the time you have washed, dressed and had breakfast it has begun to rain. At last, you realize sadly that it will continue raining all day long and you will have to stay at home. But once you have made up your mind that you will not be going out, it is always easy to find interesting things to do indoors.

9. It is hard to believe that there was ever a time when there was no radio or television. How dull the world must have been! Today we are able to learn that there has been an air-crash in New Guinea almost

immediately after it happens. We can 'go' to the theatre, to a concert, or to a football match while sitting comfortably at home. On the other hand, the world must have been a quieter place before the coming of radio. It is certain, too, that people did far more things for themselves than they do now.

10. Although there is a lot to be said for travelling by ship, by car, or by train, nothing can compare with an aeroplane. You do not have to put up with rough seas, bumpy roads, or long, monotonous stretches of countryside. An aeroplane gets you to your destination quickly and comfortably. What is more, it gives you a most unusual and exciting view of the world which is far superior to anything you can see out of a car or a train window or from the deck of a ship.

Last Paragraphs

11. I left the exhibition realizing that I would have to visit it at least once again. After walking around for five hours I had still only seen a very small part of all the interesting things on display.

12. Many people find autumn beautiful. But for me the sight of yellowing leaves means one thing only: the end of summer. With the first hint of autumn I realize sadly that there are many cold bitter months ahead and it will be a long time before the carefree days of summer return once more.

13. Your first visit to a foreign country always remains a precious memory. Seen for the first time, people and places so different from your own leave a deep and lasting impression.

14. At the end of the programme everyone began clapping when the performers came on to the stage one by one. There were cheers and loud cries of 'Encore' when the magician appeared. He had been by far the most popular, for his clever tricks had both mystified and delighted the audience.

15. Moving to a new house had certainly been exhausting. I sat down and counted the damage: four broken cups, a cigarette burn in my best carpet and a table standing unsteadily on three legs. When I remembered all that had happened, I considered myself lucky to have got off so lightly!

16. As soon as I got home everybody asked me how the day had been. I still remember how anxious my mother was and all the questions she asked me. What was it like, working for the first time? Was the head-clerk really as dreadful as everyone had said he was? How did I spend the day? I was so tired, I hardly said a word and after supper I went straight to bed.

17. The most remarkable thing about him, however, was not his outstanding ability as a leader. He was a person who always had a kind word

for the humblest and who knew how to deal tactfully even with the most foolish of people. Those of us who were fortunate enough to be his friends will never forget him.

18. It is so rare to meet a true craftsman these days that I could hardly believe that each one of the beautiful objects which lay scattered carelessly on the floor, on the shelves, and even on the work-bench, had been made by hand.

19. Nobody had expected the re-union party to be such a success. Meeting old school friends again after so many years had provided many unexpected surprises. It had been such a pleasure to recall our school-days and to see faces which had once been so familiar and which now were barely recognizable.

20. The old chief was sorry to see us go. We shook hands sadly with everyone of the people who had come to say good-bye. Many of them were crying and offering us presents of fruit and nuts. From the boat we waved to them until we could see them no more. In the end, the island itself disappeared. We knew we would never forget such kind and friendly people.

First and Last Paragraphs

21. (a) Looking at an atlas has the same fascination as looking up a word in a dictionary. You try to find one thing and are soon carried away by another so that in the end you forget what it was you were originally looking for. In this way an atlas often enables us to take imaginary trips to distant places or to trace the journeys of great explorers.

(b) For some time I imagined what it must have been like to cross the Pacific in a raft. Then turning over the pages of the atlas again, I found that I was soon off on another journey.

22. (a) At about 10.30 in the morning there were signs that everybody in the city was getting restless. People would come out of shops and look up at the sky; others would stop in the middle of the street and either point or gaze upwards. To anyone that had not read in the newspaper that there would be an eclipse of the sun at 11.0 o'clock, this must have seemed very strange behaviour indeed. As the time drew near, the crowds in the street either hurried home or stood about waiting for something to happen.

(b) Soon it was day-time again, and people went about their work as if nothing had happened. The dark night in the middle of the day had passed.

23. (a) By the time we arrived, the party was in full swing. We stopped outside the dance-hall and inspected each other carefully before going in as this was no ordinary party. Everybody would be in fancy-dress and

we wanted to be quite sure that no one would recognize us. My friend, Ken, was dressed as a circus clown, and I followed close behind, dressed as a lion-tamer.

(b) It was at this point that the lights suddenly went out. From where I was, I could hear windows being opened. This was followed by screams, shouting, and laughter. When the lights came on again, we saw about ten people dressed as ghosts. They were all walking slowly towards us with their arms outstretched!

24. (a) The hut had taken the boys months to build. The site for it had been carefully selected. It was at the top of a grassy slope overlooking the village in the valley below. Near by there was a farm so that the boys had a plentiful supply of fresh water. Every spare moment after school had been spent on building the hut. Now that it was complete, it resembled a small cottage.

(b) The boys often spent the night there in sleeping-bags. They would light a camp-fire and prepare their own food. As the lights of the houses in the village began to go out, they would return to the little hut they had built.

25. (a) Auction sales in our village attract a very strange crowd. Most people go out of curiosity and very few of them have any serious intention of buying anything. Week after week one sees the same old faces waiting expectantly for the sale to begin. In a quiet village there can hardly be a more pleasant way of spending an afternoon.

(b) The last item up for sale was an ancient lawn-mower. Not expecting that anybody would be interested in buying it, the auctioneer offered it for the modest sum of five pence. Without a moment's hesitation, the man in the green suit raised his hand yet again, much to the delight of everybody present. The man had certainly bought the strangest collection of things!

26. (a) Our new neighbours moved in last week when we were away on holiday. The old house next door looked so different when we first saw it. There were curtains in the windows; smoke was rising from the chimneys; the hedge round the garden had been clipped; and the old, weather-beaten verandah had been given a coat of paint.

(b) It had not taken long for us to become friends. In a short time we were talking as if we had known each other for years. We went home thinking what a pleasure it was to have neighbours again, for the house next door had been vacant for over a year.

27. (a) Last night it was announced on the radio that the famous comedian, Billy Hall, had decided to spend the night alone in the waxworks museum. He would be sleeping in the gallery where the figures of all the most dreadful criminals of the past and present were on display. The announcer said that listeners would be taken over to Mr Hall every half-hour to hear an account of his impressions.

(b) 'The time is now twelve o'clock and this is my last report for the
night,' continued the voice of Mr Hall. 'I wish I could think of something
funny to say, but I'm afraid my sense of humour seems to have deserted
me. I keep telling myself that, after all, they're only made of wax, but
it's often hard to believe. Well, good-night, listeners. I do hope you hear
from me again in the morning! Good-night!'

28. (a) I love sitting out in the garden on a summer's day and watching
the ants. Never once are they tempted to laze in the warm sun and think
of nothing in particular. I do not think I admire them for this, but I
certainly find it interesting to see them dealing with big problems.
The other day, for instance, I looked on (without helping them even
once) as they performed a task fit for Hercules: they successfully
carried an enormous dead beetle home over a distance of about five
yards.

(b) The beetle disappeared down the ant-hole followed by hundreds
of triumphant ants. It was amazing to think that in human terms the
ants had climbed two mountains, crossed a river, and penetrated a thick
forest while carrying such a huge load. And all this was done in less
than an hour!

29. (a) The worst time to travel in the city is between 7.30 and 9.0
o'clock in the morning and 5.0 and 7.0 o'clock in the evening. At these
times everybody is either going to or coming from work and is in a
dreadful hurry. No matter how frequently trains or buses arrive there
are always more than enough people to fill them.

(b) These are just a few of the reasons why you should avoid travelling
during what is called the 'rush hour'. At this time every day even the
shortest of journeys is unpleasant and exhausting.

30. (a) The workmen shouted excitedly and the archaeologist came
hurrying over: the men had dug up some ancient steps which had been
hidden for centuries. Little by little, they carefully cleared away the hard
soil. Everyone was silent and breathless when the steps were found to lead
to the sealed door of a tomb.

(b) The door of the tomb was closed again and two workmen were
posted outside it to keep watch all night. Before leaving, the archaeologist
gave them strict orders that no one was to be allowed near until he
returned early next day with a team of photographers and experts.

Narrative and descriptive: a hundred ideas

Instructions

Write essays of between 250 and 350 words on each of the following
subjects. You should spend about an hour and a quarter on each essay.
The best way to divide your time is as follows: plan: 10–15 minutes;

writing: 45–50 minutes; re-reading: 10–15 minutes. Where necessary, give your essay a title.

1. Suppose you overheard two thieves talking. Write an account of what they said.
2. Pages from a diary.
3. A story about a man who tried to have 'a free ride' on a train. Describe his efforts to avoid the ticket collector.
4. Describe the radio or televison programme you enjoy listening to most and say why you find it interesting.
5. Give an account of an afternoon you spent trying to entertain a young nephew who was not easily amused.
6. Unusual means of transport.
7. An amusing story about an absent-minded person.
8. Our English teacher.
9. A story about a miser who suspects that his next-door neighbour knows where he hides his money.
10. The conquest of space.
11. A mysterious telephone call and what it led to.
12. A snow-storm.
13. A story called 'The Terrible Twins'.
14. Describe the main street in your city, town, or village on a busy morning.
15. An amusing story about a driving test. Imagine that the person driving the car has already failed five times.
16. An account of yourself as you think your best friend sees you.
17. An imaginary journey in a balloon.
18. An imaginary description of a swarm of locusts descending on a big farm.
19. A story called 'Adventure in a Taxi'.
20. A typical day in the year 2070.
21. A story about some hunters who attempt to catch a rhinoceros alive.
22. Caught in the rain.
23. Imagine you were travelling in the same train-compartment as a madman. Describe what happened.
24. Describe the interval at the theatre or at a concert.
25. A story called 'Buried Alive'.
26. Describe the people you might see waiting for a train at a big railway station.
27. A story called 'The Merry Millionaire'.
28. The man or woman you would like to marry.
29. Some relatives whom you do not very much want to see arrive from the country or city and decide to spend a week with you.

30. A discussion between two old men who are recalling 'the good old days'.
31. A fable of your own in which the animals speak and act like human beings. In this case however, all the usual qualities given to animals could be reversed (e.g. the sheep could be cunning and deceitful; the fox stupid; the wolf tame etc.).
32. Sleeping in the open.
33. A story about two prisoners of war who escape from enemy territory disguised as peasants.
34. Human beings seen from the point of view of a monkey in a cage at the zoo.
35. A story called: 'The Machine That Went Mad'.
36. Your favourite view in the country near your home.
37. You have been receiving a number of anonymous letters (unpleasant or funny). Write a story showing how you came to discover who the writer was.
38. Your most embarrassing experience.
39. The magazine you like best.
40. A story about a dangerous criminal who is supposed to be hiding in a quiet village.
41. Saturday afternoon.
42. A story about a snob.
43. A visit to a circus.
44. Your home and family first thing on Monday morning.
45. The crowd outside a cinema.
46. 'If I were Prime Minister ...'
47. Describe what you would most like a foreign visitor to your country to see.
48. 'He who laughs last, laughs best.' Write a story about a practical joker who plays one joke too many.
49. The time I was ill.
50. A story entitled: 'Mountain Rescue'.
51. Describe your town or village as it was a hundred years ago.
52. A detailed account of an exciting football match or motor rally.
53. If walls could speak ...
54. Imagine a day you spent as an assistant in a shoe shop.
55. What the world would be like without oil
56. A very ordinary dog called 'Mutt' becomes hero.
57. A trip down a big river by boat.
58. When you return home late one night you find that a thief has entered your house. You are soon led to suspect that he is still hiding somewhere in the house. Describe how he is caught.
59. A fashion show.

60. A story called 'Arctic Winter'.
61. Some interesting new inventions.
62. A fairy story about a witch and a soldier.
63. A 'blurb' is a short account of a book usually printed on the dust cover. Write a 'blurb' about a novel called 'The Unfortunate Traveller'.
64. A journey over Everest in an aeroplane.
65. A story about a person who tried to cheat the Customs and was caught.
66. A thunderstorm.
67. A story about a landlady who is always reading detective stories. One night she is reading in bed as usual when one of her lodgers comes home rather late. In the dark she mistakes him for a thief and ...
68. A seaside holiday.
69. A story called: 'The Man Who Knew Everything'
70. Imagine yourself in the position of a bus-conductor writing of the things you dislike most.
71. The day an ancient motor-car held up the traffic.
72. A visit to a factory.
73. A story about a stowaway who hides in a life-boat. He is discovered when, during the journey, the boat has to be lowered into the sea.
74. A visit to a country fair.
75. A story called : 'Counterfeit Money'.
76. Our national characteristics.
77. An unusual day in the life of a dust-man.
78. Your class as you think your teacher sees it.
79. The choice of a job or a profession.
80. A story about how a doctor or a nurse deals with a difficult patient who imagines he is ill when there is nothing the matter with him.
81. Describe what you consider to be the ideal way to bring up children.
82. A story about a photographer working for a newspaper who manages to take some astonishing photographs of a big building which is on fire at night.
83. An amusing account of a foolish person who believed everything he was told.
84. My parents.
85. A crowd is watching an air-display. One or more of the planes gets into serious difficulties. Describe what the crowd saw.
86. Where I would like to live if I had to emigrate.
87. Imagine you are being followed. Write a story describing how you managed to get away from your pursuers (or describing how you were finally caught).

88. A day in the life of a hotel booking-clerk.
89. A story entitled 'Trapped in a Mine'.
90. The indoor game you like best.
91. Sunrise.
92. Describe how you would plan a garden.
93. Write a story about some street musicians who disturb a quiet neighbourhood early one Sunday morning.
94. Imagine a journey into a remote jungle where you meet some stone-age dwellers who have never before seen people from the outside world.
95. A story called: 'The Frightened Ghost'.
96. My first cigarette.
97. Describe the changes that have been made in your town or village since World War II.
98. A story about a boastful person who (as events prove) is not quite so able as he thinks he is.
99. Imagine a day on earth before the arrival of man.
100. An earthquake.

Letter-writing

Lay-out

General Information

1. LAY-OUT All letters in English are arranged (or *laid out*) on paper according to a certain plan. The word 'lay-out' is used when we refer to this general arrangement.

2. THE HEADING This term refers to the address which appears at the top (or *head*) of the letter. The address is written in the top right-hand corner of the page and is followed by the date. There are two forms: the 'Indented Style' and the 'Block Style'. Either form may be used.

Here is an example of the 'Indented Style':

> 14 Penrose St.,
> Reading,
> Berks.,
> England.
> March 4th, 19—

This is the 'Block Style':

> 14 Penrose St.,
> Reading,
> Berks.,
> England.
> March 4th, 19—

Some Points to Note:

(a) Notice that the order of the address is as follows: number of house, name of street, town or city, area, country. Never write your own name at the top of the letter.

(b) Pay special attention to the punctuation. Notice that there is a comma after each line and a full stop after the last one.

(c) Note that the abbreviation for 'street' in English is 'St.' not 'Str.' Other abbreviations are: 'Rd.' (Road), 'Sq.' (Square), 'Ave.' (Avenue), 'Pl.' (Place). Words like 'Drive' or 'Lane' are not abbreviated.

(d) The date is written in full, i.e.: 9th Feb., 19—. The months of the year which may be abbreviated are: 'Jan.', 'Feb.', 'Aug.', 'Sept.', 'Oct.', 'Nov.', 'Dec.'. The abbreviations used for days are: 1st, 2nd, 3rd, 4th etc. These numbers may be placed either before or after the name of the month: e.g. 'June 8th' and '8th June' are equally correct.

(e) The name of the country may be left out of your address only when you are writing to someone who lives in your own country.

3. THE MARGIN Make sure that there is a clear margin on the left-hand side and that you leave an equal amount of space on the right. Your letter must appear in the middle of the page, not on one side.

4. THE SALUTATION This word is used when we speak of the actual beginning of the letter. Most letters should be begun with the word 'Dear' which should be written against the left-hand margin.

5. THE BODY The letter itself is usually referred to as the *body*. This is the main part of the lay-out. Make sure that each paragraph is indented correctly and that you start each following line against the left-hand margin.

6. THE SUBSCRIPTION This term is used when we refer to the end of the letter. The subscription is begun with the word 'Yours'. (Note that the 'Y' is a capital letter and that there is no apostrophe before the 's'.)

7. THE SIGNATURE This should come underneath the subscription and should always be written clearly.

8. THE POSTSCRIPT If you wish to say something more after you have finished your letter, you may add a few lines under the signature. What you add must be headed with the letters 'P.S.' which is the abbreviated form of 'Postscript'.

The personal letter

Instructions

1. When writing to friends, make every effort to be natural. If you have to give reasons for something, make sure that they are convincing. Each time you write, try to imagine you are writing a *real* letter, not just an exercise.

2. THE SALUTATION Never begin 'Dear Friend'. You should address your friends by their Christian names: i.e. 'Dear Tom', 'Dear Jane' etc. When writing to relations you may address them as 'Dear Uncle Tom' or 'Dear Aunt Jane' but never 'Dear Cousin' or 'Dear Cousin George'. If you are writing a friendly letter to persons with whom you are not on Christian-name terms you should address them as 'Dear Mr (or Mrs, or Miss) Johnson'. A letter to a person with whom you are on very friendly terms may be begun 'My dear'. The name in the Salutation is always followed by a comma.

3. THE BODY In the short letters you will be expected to write, the body has three main parts:

| Introduction | Purpose | Conclusion |

(a) *Introduction* You should begin your letter by referring either to a letter you have recently received, or to an event which has prompted you to write.

Here are a few useful phrases:

I have just this moment received your letter and am writing at once because ...

I am sorry it has taken me so long to reply to your last letter but ...

Thank you so much for answering my letter so quickly.

What a surprise it was to get a letter from you after all this time!

How nice it was to hear from you at last.

I had given you up for lost but this morning ...

It was such a disappointment to learn ...

I was very sorry to hear ...

Whatever has become of you?

You will be very glad to hear that ...

(b) *Purpose* This is the most important part of the letter. It is here that you explain *why* you are writing. Take very great care to answer exactly the question you have been set. At the same time, include personal details which will make your letter interesting.

(c) *Conclusion* It is customary to 'round off' a letter with a polite wish. This may take any form: e.g. expressing the hope to see someone soon; sending regards; being remembered to friends etc.

Here are a few useful phrases:

I shall be looking forward to seeing/hearing from you soon.

I do hope you will soon be up and about again.

Please give my love/regards/best wishes to ...

You can be quite sure that it will never happen again!

I'll be there at six o'clock and I promise I'll really try to be punctual this time.

I hope you will soon settle down in ... (a new job, a new country, a new school etc.) and I shall be looking forward to hearing your first impressions.

I do hope you will be able to come this time.

4. THE SUBSCRIPTION This depends on how well you know the person you are writing to. The most usual subscription for friends and acquaintances is: *Yours sincerely*. You may, however, end *Yours very sincerely*, *Yours affectionately*, or simply, *Love*. Note that the words 'sincerely' 'affectionately' etc. begin with small letters and that they are *always* followed by a comma.

5. THE SIGNATURE Again depending on the relationship you may sign with your full name, your Christian name, or even a nickname. Make sure the signature can be read.

Read carefully the letters that follow, noting how they have been laid out and how they have been written.

(a) *Subject:* A letter regretting that a friend of yours cannot come with you on an excursion and expressing the hope that he will be able to come another time.

> 18 Middleton St.,
> Bloomsbury,
> London, W.C.1.
> 14th June, 19—

Dear Tom,

   Your card arrived this morning and you can imagine how disappointed I was to hear that you have caught another dreadful cold. You could at least have waited for a day or two!

   I saw Ron last night and we made final arrangements for tomorrow's excursion. We'll be setting off very early. I promise I won't oversleep this time! However nice the weather is, the trip won't be the same without you.

   I hope you won't be too miserable in bed and that you'll be able to come with us next week as usual.

> Yours sincerely,
> Jack

(b) *Subject:* Your first impressions of London shortly after your arrival.

> The Star Hotel,
> 14 Preston Ave.,
> London, S.W.5,
> England.
> 15th Aug. 19—

Dear Madeline,

   I arrived in London last night and your friend Peter met me at the station. I'm glad he was there because I don't think I should ever have found my hotel alone.

   Although I haven't seen much yet, I think I'm going to enjoy myself here. Last night Peter and I went for a 'short' walk. I had never imagined London was quite so big. We walked for over two hours and I had to take a train to get back to the hotel!

   I'll write again in a few days' time and I'm sure I'll have a lot to tell you.

> Yours sincerely,
> André

(c) *Subject:* A letter refusing an invitation to a birthday party and giving reasons.

Oaklands,
57 Fenton St.,
Guildford,
Surrey.
27th April 19—

Dear Betty,

Thank you very much for inviting me to your birthday party, but I'm afraid I shan't be able to come.

We have had so much to do at the office this week that Mr Simpson has asked me to work overtime for a few days. I promised I would and now there's nothing I can do about it. I'll be thinking of you when I'm typing piles of letters!

I hope your party is a success and I wish you many happy returns.

Yours sincerely,
Susan

P.S. I hope you manage to blow all the candles out!

Answer these questions:

1. Which of these letters employs the 'Indented Style' heading? •
2. Why is the name of the country included in the address of the second letter?
3. What does the introduction in each letter refer to?
4. How closely do these letters answer the questions set? Examine the second paragraph of each letter.
5. What personal details have been included to make the letters 'natural'?

Exercises

Instructions

Write personal letters of between 80 and 100 words on each of the subjects given below. Do not count the address, the salutation and the subscription in the total number of words.

You should not spend more than about 25 minutes on each letter. The best way to divide your time is as follows: plan: about 5 minutes; writing: about 15 minutes; re-reading: about 5 minutes.

1. You had arranged to meet a friend in town but it was quite impossible for you to be there. Explain why you were not able to meet him, apologize for the inconvenience you may have caused and suggest another meeting.
2. You have been invited to a party. Write a letter accepting the invitation and inquiring if it would be possible for you to bring a friend with you.

3. A friend who lives abroad will shortly be visiting your country and has asked you to make arrangements for his stay. Write a letter informing him of what you have done.

4. Your neighbour's dog got into your garden and spoilt some fine plants. Write a letter to your neighbour complaining about this and asking him to take steps to prevent the same thing happening again in future.

5. You received a present of some money from a relative. Write a letter thanking him or her for the present and saying what you intend to do with it.

6. You have just heard that a friend of yours has had an accident and is in hospital. Write a letter wishing him a speedy recovery and telling him that you hope to be able to visit him soon.

7. Your first letter to a 'pen-friend' in America.

8. A letter congratulating an old friend of yours who has just got engaged.

9. A letter to a friend giving him advice on what to take with him on a camping holiday.

10. You have been sent two complimentary tickets for a concert. Write a letter to a friend inviting him to come with you and telling him something about the programme.

11. You are returning a book which you borrowed from a friend. Write a letter thanking him for lending it to you and telling him how much you enjoyed it.

12. A friend has kindly offered to look after your dog while you are away on holiday. Write a letter pointing out a few things which you think he should know.

13. You have just returned home after a pleasant visit to a relation in the country. Write a letter thanking him for his hospitality and saying what you enjoyed most while you were there.

14. While travelling on a ship last summer you exchanged addresses with a person whom you had only known a short time. Write a letter giving news of yourself.

15. A friend of yours is thinking of moving into your neighbourhood. Write a letter advising him against such a move.

16. Write a letter to a friend of yours asking for a loan of some money which you urgently require. Say why you want it and when you expect to be able to return it.

17. Imagine you are at this moment travelling by air. Write a letter to a friend describing your journey.

18. While your neighbour is on holiday you accidentally break one of his windows. Write to him explaining how it happened and telling him what you have done to make good the damage.

19. Enclosed in an envelope together with a Christmas card is a letter from a friend who writes to you once a year. Answer it giving news of yourself.
20. Write a letter refusing an invitation to a party and explaining why you cannot go.
21. A friend has asked you to recommend a good car-route to a well-known resort. Write a letter giving him advice and suggesting places he should see on the way.
22. Yesterday you wrote a letter to a friend refusing an invitation to go with him to the theatre. You now find that you are free to go. Write a letter explaining how this happened and inquiring whether it will be possible to accompany him.
23. Write a letter to a relation who has written to you complaining that you never write to him.
24. Write a letter to your mother telling her how much you are enjoying your holiday abroad.
25. Write a letter to a friend describing your new job.
26. Write a letter to an old person of eighty-one congratulating him on his birthday.
27. Write a letter to a friend with whom you have quarrelled suggesting that you should both forget all about it and asking him if he would care to meet you.
28. Write a letter to an unpleasant person whom you believe has spread rumours about you which are untrue.
29. A friend of yours has written to you congratulating you on your success in your examinations. Write a reply regretfully informing him that you failed.
30. A friend is due to arrive in a few days with his family for a visit. Write a letter telling him not to come because one of your children has measles.
31. You have just heard that a friend of yours will be travelling abroad by car. Write a letter asking him whether it would be possible to accompany him and offering to share expenses.
32. You have inherited a big sum of money from an old aunt who died recently. Write a letter to a friend about the good news and telling him what you intend to do with the money.
33. Write a letter you would not like to receive.
34. Write a letter to a friend in the country who is thinking of finding a job in town, outlining difficulties and prospects.
35. An English friend of yours always writes to you in your language and you write to him in his. Write a letter telling him whether you think he is improving or not and asking him to give you his opinion on the state of your English.

36. Write a letter to an old school-teacher briefly giving news of yourself from the time you left school.

37. Write a letter to a friend urging him to see a play which has made a big impression on you.

38. Write a letter to a friend describing how you spent Christmas.

39. A friend left his umbrella at your home on a recent visit. Write a letter informing him of this and making arrangements for its return.

40. You accidentally left the electric iron on one evening when you went out; fortunately it did not do much damage. Write an account of what happened to a friend.

41. You borrowed a gramophone record from a friend but have damaged it slightly. Write a letter informing him of what has happened and offering to replace the record.

42. A man whom you do not know at all but who is well acquainted with a friend of yours has written you a friendly letter asking you to help him find a job. Write an answer.

43. One of your friends will be visiting a distant town where an aunt of yours lives. Write a letter to your aunt introducing your friend and asking her if he could come and see her.

44. You have had to leave your lodgings unexpectedly and will be away for two weeks. Write a letter to your landlady explaining your sudden disappearance and informing her when you expect to be back.

45. An old friend whom you have not seen for ten years has suddenly arrived at your town and is staying at a hotel. Write him a letter inviting him to come and stay with you.

46. While abroad you had promised to call on an acquaintance. You now find that you do not have the time. Write a letter explaining why you cannot keep your promise and apologizing.

47. You have been elected to play for your local football team. Write to a friend telling him about this and asking him to be present at your first game.

48. You have heard that a very unpleasant person intends to pay an unexpected visit on a very close friend of yours. Write a letter to your friend warning him about this.

49. You should have written a letter to a relation long ago to thank him or her for a present but you forgot. Write a letter of thanks in which you apologize for the delay in answering.

50. Answer a letter from a little boy who has asked you to send him stamps for his collection.

The business letter
Instructions

1. There is no such thing as 'business English'. In the past business letters were full of such meaningless phrases as 'esteemed inquiry', I enclose herewith', 'We have perused', 'I beg to acknowledge', 'your earliest convenience', 'I hope I may be favoured' etc. You may very occasionally come across bad letters written today which contain phrases of this sort. *Never* attempt to imitate this style of writing. Your language should be simple and clear.

2. THE HEADING This differs in one important detail from the personal letter. The name and address of the person you are writing to must be included beneath your own address but against the *left*-hand margin. This is called the 'Inside Address' and should be exactly the same as the one which will appear on the envelope. If you are writing to a man, his name should appear as 'Mr E. Jones' or 'E. Jones Esq.' (Esquire). This latter form of address is in general use and is usually preferable. When writing to ladies the usual title is used: i.e.: 'Mrs J. Robinson' or 'Miss J. Robinson'.

Very often you will not know the name of the person who will read your letter. In this case you may address your letter directly to the company concerned: e.g. Jones, Brown and Co., Ltd., ('Co.' and 'Ltd.' are the usual abbreviations for 'Company' and 'Limited'.) When you are writing to a particular person in a Company or other organization and do not know his or her name, your letter may be addressed to 'The Manager', 'The Director', 'The Principal', 'The Headmaster', 'The Secretary' etc. as the case may be.

In business letters the 'Block Style' of address is becoming more common and should be preferred.

3. THE SALUTATION If the person you are writing to is known to you, you may begin 'Dear Mr —', 'Dear Mrs —', etc. In all other instances, you should begin 'Dear Sir,', 'Dear Sirs,', or 'Dear Madam,' 'Gentlemen' or 'Sirs' as the case may be.

4. THE BODY A business letter usually has four main parts:

    Reference
    Information
    Purpose
    Conclusion

(a) *Reference* You should begin your letter by referring to a letter you have received, an advertisement you have seen etc., or to an event which has prompted you to write.

Here are a few useful phrases:

Thank you for your letter of June 3rd.

Many thanks for your letter of April 24th.

In your letter of May 22nd you inquire about ...

It was a great pleasure to receive your letter of Nov. 7th.

I was very sorry to learn from your letter of June 22nd that ...

In reply to your inquiry of Oct. 21st, I regret that ...

I read your advertisement in last Monday's issue of 'The Commercial Gazette' and ...

You may remember that I visited you last year when I was in ...

I was surprised to learn that ...

I recently attended Hanover Fair and ...

I recently called on your agent in this country to ask about ... but he was unable to help me.

(b) *Information* In the second paragraph it is sometimes necessary to supply more detailed information which is related to the 'Reference'.

(c) *Purpose* Here you must give the reason why you are writing your letter. You should state clearly what you want. Take care to answer closely the question that has been set.

(d) *Conclusion* As in the 'Personal Letter' it is customary to 'round the letter off' with some polite remark.

Here are a few useful phrases:

I am looking forward to hearing from you soon.

I sincerely hope you will be able to help me in this matter.

I enclose a sample of the material you require.

I do hope I am not putting you to too much trouble.

I shall not act until I have received instructions from you.

I would greatly appreciate an early reply.

I enclose a cheque for £5 to cover costs.

Would you please let me know as soon as possible whether you would be willing to ...

I would suggest that you come and see me in person on ...

Please accept my apologies for the trouble this mistake has caused you.

5. *The Subscription* Where a letter is begun Dear Sir/Sirs/Madam, you must end with the words 'Yours faithfully'. When, however, you address a person by name – even if you barely know him – you must conclude with the words 'Yours sincerely'.

6. THE SIGNATURE Sign your name clearly *in full* in the way you wish it to appear on the envelope which will be addressed to you in reply to your letter.

A few of the most common forms of business letter are given below. Read them carefully noting how they have been laid out and how they have been written.

(a) *The Letter of Inquiry*

Subject: A letter to a hotel abroad booking a room for a short stay and inquiring about the cost.

104 Avenue des Alpes,
Zurich,
Switzerland.
18th May 19—

The Manager,
Park Hotel,
Brighton,
England.

Dear Sir,

I am writing at the suggestion of a friend who stayed at your hotel last year and has warmly recommended it to me.

I expect to arrive in Brighton on June 23rd and would like a single room with a private bath. I shall be staying for five days and would like to have all my meals at your hotel.

Would you please let me know whether you have a room available and how much my stay is likely to cost?

I shall be looking forward to hearing from you soon.

Yours faithfully,
Albert Durant

Subject: A letter from someone intending to open a book-shop and inquiring about the possibility of obtaining rare books.

227 Solonos St.,
Kolonaki,
Athens,   -
Greece.
24th Nov. 19—

A. L. Harrison Esq.,
'The Book Shop',
27 Newcombe Road,
Finsbury Park,
London, N.4,
England.

Dear Mr Harrison,

I have been studying the rare-book catalogue you gave me while I was in London and I feel that there would be considerable demand here for many of the books on your list.

By mid-December I shall have opened a book-shop of my own in which I hope to sell rare books. Would you please let me know whether you would be prepared to keep me supplied with books published in the early seventeenth century? I would also like to know whether lots 73 and 97 in your catalogue are still available.

My kindest regards to your wife,

Yours sincerely,
D. Lambros

(b) *The Letter of Complaint*
Subject: A letter complaining about a tape-recorder which arrived
badly damaged.

> P. O. Box 97431,
> Nairobi,
> Kenya,
> East Africa.
> 19th Jan. 19—

D. West and Co., Ltd.,
Electrical Supplies,
57 Amhurst Crescent,
London, S.W.3,
England.

Dear Sirs,
    The tape-recorder No. JB/4703/08 which I ordered from you on
Nov. 17th arrived last night.
    I very much regret to have to inform you that the machine has been
badly damaged. When I opened the packing-case I found that the lid
of the recorder had been cracked and the surface of the machine has been
scratched.
    Would you please let me know whether you would be willing to send
me a new recorder and if I should arrange to return the damaged one to
you.
    In the meantime, I shall hold on to the machine you sent until I hear
from you.

> Yours faithfully,
> J. T. Edwards

(c) *The Letter of Application for a Post*
Subject: A letter applying for the post of air-hostess.

> 596 Friedrich St.,
> Hanover.
> 14th Sept. 19—

The Employment Officer,
Home and Overseas Airways Ltd.,
Sigmund House,
79 Bremen St.,
Hanover.

Dear Sir,
    I was interested to read in your magazine, 'Go by Air', that you
require air-hostesses.

I am nineteen years old and am at present attending the Modern Languages School at 24 Lowen St. where I am studying English and French. I have been there since leaving the State Realschule three years ago.

I wish to apply for a post as air-hostess and am free to attend for interview on any day except Mondays and Fridays.

The Principal of my present school, Mr T. Jones, and my old head-master, Herr G. Schultz, have kindly agreed to send information about me if you require it.

Yours faithfully,
Else Klein

Answer these questions:

1. In what ways do the inside addresses and salutations differ from each other?
2. Why does the subscription of the second letter differ from the others?
3. Show how the body of each letter follows the pattern: Reference, Information, Purpose, Conclusion. Which of the four letters does not follow this scheme exactly? Why not?
4. How closely does each letter answer the question?
5. Would you say that the language used is direct and clear? Justify your answer.

Exercises

Instructions

Write business letters of between 80 and 100 words on each of the subjects given below. Do not count the address, the salutation and the subscription in the total number of words.

You should not spend more than about 25 minutes on each letter. The best way to divide your time is as follows: plan: about 5 minutes; writing: about 15 minutes; re-reading: about 5 minutes.

1. You have been invited by the librarian of your local library to give a talk in English to a small audience. Write a letter refusing the invitation.
2. You are opening a shop in your town and would like to act as chief representative of an English clothing firm which you know has no agents in your country. Write a letter offering to act as agent and outlining your qualifications.
3. Write a letter to a tourist agency on behalf of a club you belong to. You want to know whether it will be possible for twenty members

of your club to travel abroad by coach and whether the agency can make arrangements for transport, accommodation etc.

4. You ordered a new car from England but when it arrived you discovered that there was no spare wheel in the boot. Write a letter pointing this out and requesting that a spare wheel be sent immediately, by air if possible.

5. Write to your previous employer or old headmaster requesting that he act as referee on your behalf to support your application to work as draughtsman for a big firm abroad.

6. An English firm has written to you inquiring about goods which you supply. Answer the inquiry stating how much the goods cost, when they can be delivered and what your terms of payment are.

7. Write a letter to an English factory cancelling an order which you made for some machinery. Your reason for doing so is that your business has not been doing very well lately.

8. A famous English writer has arrived in your town. Write him a letter asking him to give a talk to your school about his impressions of your country.

9. You have read an advertisement in a newspaper for a secretary who would be willing to travel abroad. Write a letter stating your qualifications and applying for the position.

10. Some goods you ordered from abroad have failed to arrive. Write a letter to the firm concerned in which you point out how much difficulty this delay is causing you and requesting that the goods be sent as soon as possible.

11. You wish to deposit money in a bank abroad. Write a letter to your local bank asking for information about how this can be done.

12. Write a letter to a car-insurance firm making a claim for damages after a recent accident you had while driving abroad.

13. You hold the position of secretary of a local football club but now wish to resign. Write a letter to the manager of the club giving your reasons for wishing to do so.

14. Write a letter to your local post-office notifying your change of address and requesting that any mail for you be re-directed.

15. While travelling abroad, a suit-case of yours was lost at a railway station. Write a letter to the Station-master inquiring whether it has been found and asking whether it could be sent to your present address.

16. You will not be able to attend English lessons because your firm is sending you to a provincial town for a fortnight. Write to the Principal of the school informing him of this and stating when you hope to resume studies.

17. You urgently require spare parts for machinery. Write to a firm in England asking where their representatives are in your country.
18. A typewriter you ordered has arrived but has been damaged in transit. Write a letter to the firm concerned pointing this out and asking what action they propose to take.
19. An engineering firm in your country has invited applications in English from engineers. Write a letter stating your qualifications and applying for a post.
20. You bought some tickets from an airline company to travel by air but now find that you will be unable to do so. Write a letter inquiring whether the tickets may be returned.
21. The B.B.C. has invited comments on one of its programmes from listeners abroad. Write a letter in reply to this request.
22. Write to an English publishing firm asking for a catalogue of their latest publications.
23. You booked a room at a hotel abroad but now find that you will be unable to travel. Write a letter cancelling your reservation.
24. An organization abroad has offered scholarships for those wishing to study languages at a university. Write a letter stating your qualifications and requesting that an application form be sent to you.
25. The director of your firm will shortly be travelling abroad. As his private secretary, write a letter on his behalf to a travel agency requesting that they reserve a berth on a ship.
26. You wish to attend a summer school abroad to study art. Write a letter applying for a place and requesting that a prospectus be sent to you. Inquire also what arrangements will be made about accommodation.
27. You wish to send your son or daughter to a school abroad. Write a letter to an educational agency stating the sort of school you require and asking whether they could act as guardians on your behalf.
28. Just before leaving your country for a holiday abroad, you insured your luggage at a railway station. While you were on holiday one of your cases was stolen. Write to the insurance company making a claim.
29. Some goods you ordered have arrived but they are not up to their usual standard. Write to the firm concerned complaining about this and asking what action they propose to take.
30. You wish to take part in an international art competition. Write to the organization concerned asking for information.
31. You wrote a letter to a firm complaining that some goods you had ordered had failed to reach you. Just after you sent the letter the goods in question arrived. Write to the firm pointing this out.
32. You ordered some books from a bookshop and enclosed a cheque.

Some time later you received a letter from the shop demanding payment for the books. Write a letter pointing out that they have made a mistake.

33. You are applying for the position of interpreter to a firm which has requested that all applications should be written in English. Write stating your qualifications.

34. Write a letter to the B.B.C. placing an order for its weekly radio programme for overseas listeners called *London Calling*.

35. A foreigner has written to you inquiring about a flat you wish to let. Write an answer to this inquiry.

36. Write a letter placing an order for a magazine which is published abroad.

37. You read an advertisement in a newspaper that an English family are willing to place their house at the disposal of a family overseas for the holidays in return for the same favour. Write a letter to the family concerned describing your house and asking for information about theirs.

39. Write a letter to an English-language newspaper published in your country complaining about an article you read recently.

39. You lost a book which you had borrowed from a local British or American library. Write a letter pointing this out and offering to replace the book.

40. You ordered an expensive fountain-pen from a company abroad. When it arrived you were asked to pay duty which you considered to be out of proportion to the value of the pen. Write to the company informing them that you have made arrangements for the return of the pen and apologizing for the inconvenience.

41. You recently attended a lecture given by a distinguished visiting historian. Write him a letter expressing your appreciation.

42. You wish to study at a university overseas. Write a letter to the Registrar giving a brief account of yourself and inquiring whether you would be eligible for entry.

43. Write a letter of recommendation for an ex-employee of yours who has applied for a position with a firm abroad.

44. While in England you paid a visit to an English school. Write a letter of thanks to the Headmaster for all he did to make your visit interesting.

45. The manager of a hotel at a well-known seaside resort has written to you stating that all the rooms at his hotel have been booked for the season. Write a letter asking him if he could possibly suggest alternative accommodation.

46. You wanted two tickets to travel by air but were unable to obtain them. You have just heard from a friend of yours that there have

been several last-minute cancellations. Write a letter to the air-
company asking if any of these tickets are available.

47. A letter you wrote to an English firm has not been answered.
Write another inquiring whether they received the first one and
asking them to reply as soon as possible.

48. While on holiday abroad you became ill and this has prevented you
from returning to work on time. Write to your employer explaining
the situation.

49. Write a letter to an English-language newspaper published in your
country criticizing the Local Council's efforts to improve street
lighting.

50. Write a letter to a post-office abroad asking them to retain any
letters they might receive for you until you arrive.

The literary essay (elementary)

Instructions

1. TYPE OF BOOK You should, at this stage, be reading as widely as possible both for general interest and to increase your vocabulary. At the same time, whether you are preparing for an examination or not, it is wise to devote particular attention to a small selection of books as the writing of literary essays presupposes a detailed knowledge of certain texts. You will be reading classics, modern novels, popular stories, plays and non-fiction – principally short biographies of famous people or accounts of exploits and outstanding achievements. The books you will be reading for special study will either be short original works or simplified texts of the level of Longmans' Simplified English Series or Longmans' Bridge Series.

2. SUMMARIES In order to be able to write literary essays you must know the contents of the books you are studying very well indeed. As it may not always be possible to read a book twice, it is advisable to keep a record of what you read. A well-arranged summary will enable you to revise the contents of a whole book in a matter of minutes.

It is not necessary to write long, laborious summaries of each chapter. These are tedious to write and not very exciting to read. The best way to keep a record of a book is to make a page by page summary in note form. It is rarely necessary to write more than a few points for each page. Here is an example based on the Longmans' Simplified version of *Jane Eyre*.

	Chapter 1
Page	GATESHEAD
9	Reed children: Eliza, John, Georgiana. Jane dismissed. Room next door: book, window-seat.
10	Discovered by John. Appearance: fat, coarse features. Character: selfish; ill-treats Jane.
11	Strikes and insults Jane. Throws book at her. They fight. Discovered by Mrs Reed, Bessie & Abbot. Jane punished: Red Room.

Chapter 2

THE RED ROOM

13   Attitude of maids: both against Jane.

14   Jane locked in room. Remembers kind uncle and the promise Mrs Reed had made to him.

15   Thinks of the dead: light, 'ghost'. She screams. Attracts attention but Mrs Reed refuses to let her out.

This sort of summary tells you all you need to know and the page-references enable you to look up any incident in the story which you may have forgotten. When you have finished making out your summary you are ready to begin essay writing.

3. TYPES OF ESSAY The literary essays you will be writing will be narrative and descriptive, but unlike general essays, these will be based entirely on the books you have studied. The questions you will be set will be designed to test your knowledge of the book. You may be required to reproduce in your own words any particular part of the story or to write a brief description of one or more characters.

4. ANSWERING THE QUESTION You may know the contents of a book very well and yet still fail to write a satisfactory essay. It is most important to discipline yourself to answer each question *as closely as possible*. Do not disregard the question altogether and then proceed to tell the whole story from the beginning to impress on the reader the fact that you know the book well. You must only include information which helps you to answer the question.

5. ACCURACY All the information given in your essay about characters and events should be accurate. There should be no difficulty about this if you know the book well. On no account attempt to 'invent' facts of your own or to write things about the characters which are not in the book. It is not necessary to learn passages by heart in order to be able to quote. If, however, you do quote a phrase, make sure you are using the *exact* words of the book. Do not put quotation marks around words or phrases which were never spoken at all but which have occurred to you on the spur of the moment.

6. REPRODUCING PART OF THE STORY If you are asked to re-tell part of the story in your own words, take great care to relate events in the order in which they occurred. When arranging your facts in chronological order you will not only avoid confusion, but you will be able to give a clear account of what happened without omitting any important details.

Some questions require a detailed knowledge of a small part of the book, say a chapter or even a fairly short scene. Do not attempt this type

of question unless you know the book well enough to be able to recon-
struct the scene, stage by stage, as it appears in the book. If a question
covers a great many chapters it is not necessary to give too much detail
about any one particular scene: keep to the most important events only.

7. 'CHARACTER' QUESTIONS Questions which require you to give an
account of a person's character are, on the whole, more difficult than
those which ask you to reproduce a scene. The reason for this is that to
answer 'character' questions you have to select your facts from all
parts of the book.

The characters in a story can be divided into two groups: the people
who play a leading part (these are called *major* characters) and those who
play a small part (*minor* characters). For instance, in *Jane Eyre*, Jane and
Mr Rochester are major characters; Mrs Reed and Grace Poole are
minor characters.

The best way to write an account of a person's character is to note
down abstract qualities which he or she possesses and then to illustrate
them by referring to events from the book. The sort of qualities you should
look for are: courage, cowardice, generosity, meanness, kindness,
cruelty, understanding, initiative, wickedness, stupidity, cunning etc.

If you are asked to give an account of the part played by a certain
person (this is not a 'character' question exactly) you should begin
with a brief and very general description of his or her character. Then
you should go on to relate the main things the person did, illustrating
your answer from your knowledge of the story.

8. PLANNING Never attempt to answer a literary question without first
making out a plan. Only by doing so will you be able to make sure that
you will answer the question closely. Once written, a plan should help
you greatly for you will know beforehand not only what you will write in
each paragraph but how many paragraphs will be included in your
essay.

A good way to make a plan is to leave a wide margin on the left-hand
side of the page. In the left-hand column you should write down any
points that will help you to answer the question. These points may be
written in any order as they occur to you. You may then order them
correctly in the right-hand column, dividing your material into clear
paragraphs. Cross out your plan neatly with a single line when you have
completed it so that it will be possible for your teacher to refer to it if
necessary.

Examine carefully the plans that follow, noting how they have been
written. They are based on questions on *Jane Eyre*.

(a) SUBJECT: Give an account of the visit of the Fortune Teller.

IDEAS	PLAN
Asks for Jane.	*Introduction*
Mary Ingram, Amy and	1. Witch's arrival: effect on guests.
Louisa Eshton.	Blanche insists.
Blanche insists.	*Development*
Witch's arrival.	2. Blanche's visit: disappointment; Mary
Mason.	Ingram, Amy and Louisa Eshton. Witch
Jane's attitude:	wants Jane.
suspicious.	3. Witch's appearance: dress, hat. Jane
Appearance of witch.	suspicious and not afraid. Crosses palm.
'Reads' her face.	4. Speaks of Blanche (loves his purse).
Crosses palm.	'Reads' Jane's face: eyes, mouth,
Eyes, forehead, mouth.	forehead.
Mr R's purse.	*Conclusion*
Reveals himself.	5. Reveals himself, asks for forgiveness.
	Jane shocks him: Mason.

(b) SUBJECT: Describe the character of Helen Burns.

IDEAS	PLAN
Contentment.	*Introduction*
Illness.	1. Who Helen Burns was: her character
Kindness.	in general: kindness, courage, influence on
Advises Jane about	Jane.
Mrs Reed.	*Development*
Punishment.	2. *Kindness:* answers questions of
Miss Scatcherd:	unknown girl (first meeting). Smiles at
history lesson.	Jane: Mr B's visit.
First meeting with Jane.	3. *Courage:* history class; accepts
Clever.	punishment without complaint (Miss
Mr Brocklehurst's visit.	Scatcherd).
Brave.	4. *Understanding:* older than Jane; advice
Miss Temple.	and influence (Mrs Reed).
Death.	5. *Cleverness:* top of class; criticizes herself,
	wants to improve; discussions with Miss
	Temple.
	Conclusion
	6. Illness and death: calm acceptance;
	Jane's sorrow.

The essay that follows is based on the second of the two plans given above. Read it carefully, noting how it has been written.

Helen Burns was the only true childhood friend Jane Eyre ever had. Her kindness and courage, her understanding and intelligence made a deep and lasting impression on the younger girl.

Jane met Helen shortly after her arrival from Gateshead. Helen was kind to her right from the start. She willingly put aside the book she was reading to answer Jane's childish questions about Lowood Institution and the staff. On a later occasion when Jane was publicly humiliated by Mr Brocklehurst, Helen smiled at her and this simple act helped Jane to face up to her punishment.

Helen herself was often punished. Once she was dismissed from a history lesson and made to stand in the middle of the classroom. Another time she was severely beaten by Miss Scatcherd. Even though the punishment was unjust, Helen accepted it without complaint.

Her belief that it was wrong to remember past injustices made Helen act in this way. When Jane complained of Mrs Reed's harsh treatment, Helen showed great understanding, but at the same time, she pointed out that people should love their enemies because nothing could be achieved by violence.

Though Helen was very clever and top of her class, she continually criticized herself in an effort to correct her 'faults'. Jane was present when Helen and Miss Temple talked together over tea. She was amazed to discover that Helen had read so much and was able to converse so well with her teacher. Moments like these were the happiest in Helen's life.

After a long illness, Helen was able to meet death with the same calm acceptance that she faced life. She died happy with no regrets. Jane, who was with Helen on the night of her death, lost a true and dear friend.

Answer these questions:

1. Would you say that the question has been answered closely? Why?
2. Show how facts are drawn from different parts of the book in order to answer the question.
3. Is all the information that is given accurate? Justify your answer from your knowledge of the story.
4. How does the writer illustrate abstract qualities of character by referring to events in the book?
5. What relationship is there between the plan and the essay. Comment on the arrangement of material.
6. In what important ways does this essay differ from one requiring you to reproduce part of the story?

Exercises

Instructions

The questions given below should be answered with reference to any books you have studied in detail. You should write essays of between 250 and 300 words not spending more than 35 minutes on each question. The best way to divide your time is as follows: plan: 5–10 minutes; writing 20–25 minutes; re-reading: 5 minutes.

1. Give a detailed account of any short scene.
2. Describe a meeting that took place between two characters and show what it led to.
3. Give a general account of the experiences of any *one* major character.
4. Write short notes on any *two* minor characters describing the part they played in the story.
5. Give an account of the part played in the story by either a major or a minor character.
6. Explain how an important event came about.
7. Give an account of a character's first impressions of a place or of other characters.
8. Describe a typical day in the life of any *one* character.
9. Explain a character's attitude to someone or something.
10. What special qualities are shown by a major or minor character (e.g. courage, initiative etc.) and how are these brought out in the story?
11. Explain the strange behaviour of a character, illustrating your answer from the story.
12. Give an account of friendship or hostility between two characters.
13. On what occasions is a person's true character revealed? Confine your answer to a consideration of any *one* major character.
14. Show how one character's suspicions of another are confirmed by the events which take place.
15. Describe an important visit that takes place in the story.

The short story

Instructions

Considered at an advanced level, narrative is an extremely difficult form of writing for which no mechanical formula can be given. A good story, however, has certain requirements which you should be well aware of before beginning to write.

1. TYPES It could be said that all fiction may be divided into two distinct categories: stories which have an entertainment-value only and which for the sake of clarification we may call 'entertainments'; and those which have an underlying purpose beyond that of merely entertaining the reader which we may call 'fables'.

(a) *Entertainments* In these, the writer makes it his aim to divert the reader pleasantly by telling him a tale. This is 'pure' fiction for the reader is expected to think only in terms of the story he is reading and not to relate it to life and to his own experiences.

(b) *Fables* Here the writer sets out with a particular theme in mind: let us say that 'knowledge is power' or that 'childhood is not the most happy and carefree period in man's life'. This is a more complicated form of story-telling in which a writer may deal with a person's state of mind or comment directly or indirectly on particular aspects of human nature. He expects the reader to see a relationship between what he reads and his own experiences or views of life in general. Behind the simple framework of the 'story' there is an *underlying theme* which all the events that take place serve to illustrate.

All stories (war stories, science fiction, ghost stories, fairy stories, stories about particular people and incidents etc.) fall into one or other of these two categories. Although some forms of story (like science fiction or detective stories) are very often 'entertainments', it is well to realize that they need not necessarily be so: they can just as easily provide the framework for a 'fable'.

2. TIME The reader must be made aware of two things: (a) Approximately when the story occurred (i.e. in our own times or in the past or future).

(b) The time covered in the story which may range from minutes to whole centuries.

3. SETTING The scene in which the story is to take place is very important since it provides a background for the events that follow. Sometimes the setting may be symbolic: for example, a living-room might symbolize isolation from the world so that it becomes something more than a mere room. Very often, too, the background setting may be an important element in the plot, equal in importance to any of the characters.

4. PLOT This is the framework of the story. It may be highly ingenious and carefully planned, or there may be no 'plot' – in the usual sense – at all. Entertainments often rely heavily on ingenious plots to keep the reader guessing and to make the story interesting. When this occurs, the framework is artificial and the writer makes every effort to provide the reader with an unexpected outcome. Fables, on the other hand, need not necessarily rely so much on plot. The writer, as it were, suddenly raises a curtain so that we can see what is going on behind it and then, equally suddenly, lets it fall.

Some of the most important elements of plot may be considered under each of the following heads: *simple or complex, beginning, middle, and end,* and *mental or physical conflict.*

(a) *Simple or Complex* A simple plot is one in which the writer concerns himself with a single main event or the fate of one or two characters. In a complex plot, however, the writer is concerned with a great number of incidents and characters. There is usually one *main situation* on which the writer makes special efforts to focus the reader's attention. The sub-plot or plots must be regarded as being subsidiary to the main plot.

(b) *Beginning, Middle, and End* This has always been and always will be a very sound foundation for any story. But as you know from modern novels and the cinema it is capable of infinite variation. You may begin in the middle and interrupt the main course of the story with one or a number of 'flash-backs' to fill in the missing parts. Or you may begin at the end and work slowly back to the beginning. You should bear in mind that it requires considerable skill – or luck – to begin in any place other than the beginning and to write a successful story.

(c) *Mental or Physical Conflict* Stories which centre upon a conflict are very exciting to read. The focal point of stories of this sort is the way the conflict is resolved, or if it is not resolved, what it is that prevents a solution.

5. DEVICES These are the means by which your story 'moves'. Here are some of them:

(a) *Foreshadowing* It is possible, early in the story, to provide hints (about characters, situations etc.) which point to the final outcome. As the story progresses, these hints become clearer to the reader. It is just as easy, of course, to side-track the reader with false hints and so deliberately mystify him.

(b) *Ingenuity in Contrivance of Effects* Above all these should be convincing; if they are not, the reader will laugh at your expense. Avoid too many 'strange coincidences'. Do not make half the characters in your story die suddenly because you can think of no better way of getting rid of them.

(c) *Journals, Letters, Diaries* This is often a good way to provide the reader with information about your characters, illuminate the past, introduce new characters, provide a 'short cut' to the solution of a conflict, introduce a new conflict, or introduce a story within a story.

(d) *Shifts in Time and Place* This should be done as smoothly as possible. There must always be some sort of link between two unrelated scenes. You must give the reader the impression that the scene he does not expect has naturally been suggested by all that has taken place so far.

6. HUMOUR

(a) *Low and High Comedy* Low comedy is the most pointed and obvious kind. It lacks subtlety but rarely fails to amuse. In the cinema it is sometimes referred to as 'slap-stick', e.g. a fat man slips on a banana skin and invariably raises a laugh. It is easy for this sort of comedy to degenerate into mere crudity. High comedy is far less obvious: it is to be found in particular situations or clever dialogue which may not at first sight seem 'funny'. A writer is capable of 'high comedy' when he realizes that there is a comic element even in the most serious or tragic moments of a man's life.

(b) *Irony and Satire* This is a form of expression in which what you write is the opposite to what you believe. Let us say that you believe that a fool should never be given a position of responsibility. You may convey this *ironically* by putting a fool in such a position and praising everything he does. Satire is a form of expression in which a writer ridicules a particular state of affairs, certain people etc. A satirist often makes great use of irony.

7. TECHNIQUE AND STYLE The degree to which the characters and the events in your story are convincing will depend on your skill or *technique*. The way you tell your story, or your *style* of writing is closely related to your technique. Characterization can be achieved by: *description, narration, dialogue, impression on others*, and *action*.

(a) *Description* Never indulge in description for its own sake: everything you describe must contribute something essential to the story. Description is usually necessary when setting a scene or giving an account of a character's physical appearance. It may be *realistic* or *impressionistic*. In realistic description, the writer describes what he sees as objectively as possible; in impressionistic description, the writer is concerned more with the effect on him of what he sees, not so much with the object itself.

(b) *Narration* The important thing in narration is the *point of view* from

which everything is seen. Here are a few things you should ask yourself:
Is the writer himself going to tell the story, and if so, in the first or the
third person? Is the writer just a story-teller, or is he an actual character
in the story? If he is just a story-teller, how aware is the reader of his
presence in the background? Is his presence desirable? Or does it prevent the reader from 'suspending his disbelief'? Is the story told from
the point of view of a character? How fair is his account of things?
Narration, as you can see, is not such a simple matter!

(c) *Dialogue* The main problem is not just that the speech should be
natural, but that each character should speak in a different way. You
must take care to provide each character with a distinct *tone of voice*.
It is possible to write a whole story in which the characters themselves
describe the setting, provide information about themselves and about
each other etc.

(d) *The Interior Monologue* This technique, frequently employed in
modern stories and novels, consists in allowing a character to 'think
aloud'. The reader then has before him the narrator's 'stream of
consciousness' (as it is sometimes called). This is a very interesting way of
presenting a story, as the character is in a position to provide information
both about himself and others in a direct manner. Shifts in time and
place are comparatively easy to manage and the plot (where there is
one) can be woven into the character's monologue.

(e) *Impression on Others* This is a subtle form of characterization in which
we learn about one character by listening to what others have to say
about him. The character concerned may then be seen in the light of
these observations so that the reader may form his own opinion of him.

(f) *Actions* A person's character may be conveyed by his actions as much
as by what the writer or anyone else has to say about him. It is possible
to let a character's actions speak for themselves so that the reader will
draw his own conclusions. Or you may consider how far a character's
actions measure up to your (or someone else's) view of him.

8. PLANNING It is very often impossible to plan a story in great detail in
the way you would an ordinary essay. But once you have decided what
type of story you are going to write, you should note a few ideas on the
plot and characters even if you find that you have to ignore them when
actually writing.

Read carefully the notes below before going on to the story that follows.

TITLE	The Record.
TYPE	An Entertainment.
TIME	The present. A few days' duration.
SETTING	Living-room. Description: realistic.

PLOT   Classical music enthusiast attempts to convert handyman.
            Record – black monkey – ludicrous results. Surprise
            ending. Beginning-middle-end sequence.
CHARACTERS Two: totally opposed in temperament but paradoxically
            friends.

The Record

Fred Ames and I haven't much in common. I sometimes wonder why
we are friends at all. Perhaps it is Fred's skill as a craftsman that I
find so attractive. He's always busy making things. Everything he makes
is so perfect that I sometimes feel a twinge of envy. If I happen to remark
that one of my books is so tattered that I shall have to throw it away,
Fred takes it home with him and returns it a few days later beautifully
bound. If I knock over a vase and it is shattered into a thousand pieces,
Fred puts it together again in such a way that only an expert would see
the difference.

My trouble is that I'm one of those hopelessly impractical and
incurably lazy people. Outside my work at the office (which is dull
enough, God knows), the only thing that interests me is listening to
classical music. I have a big collection of records and all day long the
only thing I can think about is when I am going to get home to listen to a
new symphony or concerto.

I've often tried to get Fred interested in music. When I'm in one of
my talkative moods (which isn't often, by the way), I spend hours
pointing out the beauties of a particular piece. I look at him as he's
gazing at that little black statue of a monkey I keep on the mantelpiece
and wonder if he's heard anything at all. When I look into those big,
blue, expressionless eyes of his, I realize that he hasn't been listening to a
word I've said. 'I'd love to make a copy of that some day,' he remarks,
indicating the statue.

One Saturday afternoon I came home from work even earlier than
usual. Getting home from work is one of the few things I'm good at.
It's certainly the only time I ever hurry. But this day I excelled myself.
I had just bought a new recording of Schumann's piano concerto and I
could hardly wait to listen to it.

I had already played the record twice over when Fred came in.
Perhaps because of the effect the music had on me, I was more than
usually pleased to see him. I started talking excitedly about the record:
how perfect it was, how marvellous; how he just had to listen to it. He
said nothing and after he had sat down, he asked me where the little
black monkey had got to. I answered irritably that the cleaner had
knocked it off the mantelpiece and I had thrown it away. 'What a pity,'
Fred exclaimed.

After I had put the record on, I left the living-room to make some tea. I gave Fred strict instructions to listen to the music as I was sure he would like it.

It took me some time to get the tea ready and when I returned with a tray, the second movement had just begun. I immediately started singing loudly and did not stop till the movement had come to an end. Then I remembered that I wanted Fred to listen to the concerto, not to my remarkable version of it, so I kept quiet.

Later, when I took the tea things out, I could not help thinking that there had been a different expression on Fred's face this time. His eyes had lit up in a curious way. He looked as if he had just discovered something. Once he even smiled to himself. He had been *listening*!

I got back to the living-room to find Fred actually holding the record in his hands! It was so strange to see such a delicate object in his big, rough hands that for a moment I felt like telling him to be careful. But I was too pleased with myself to do that.

'Did you enjoy it?' I asked eagerly.

'Oh, yes ... yes,' he answered vaguely.

I don't know what came over me, but at that moment I said, 'Well, you can have it.'

Fred was astonished. 'What, the record? No, I couldn't,' he answered, 'you've only just ...'

'Go on, take it!' I insisted.

'Well, thanks very much. I will.'

A few days later Fred arrived with a little box under his arm. He gave it to me smiling as soon as he came in. 'A little present,' he said.

When I opened it, I was astonished to find an exact copy of the little monkey which my cleaner had broken.

'Did you make this, Fred?' I asked incredulously.

'Yes,' answered Fred simply with a big smile all over his face.

'But however did you manage it?' I asked.

'Oh, it was quite easy really,' Fred answered. 'I got the idea from a magazine. You just melt down an old gramophone record and then you can mould it into any shape you like.'

Answer these questions:
1. Why can this story be justifiably called an entertainment?
2. How is the passage of time conveyed to the reader?
3. What is the importance of the setting? (e.g. would you say it assumes the proportion of a 'character' or not? Why?).
4. Would it be true to call the plot 'highly ingenious'? Justify your answer.
5. Is this a simple or a complex plot?

6. The story follows a beginning-middle-end pattern. What is the function of the first two paragraphs?
7. Would you say there are any elements of conflict in this story? Why?
8. Pick out instances of 'foreshadowing' which pertain to (a) the black monkey (b) Fred.
9. How does the writer deliberately mislead the reader with the contrived ending? What is the reader led to expect?
10. Is the contrivance of effects convincing? Why?
11. Pick out the comic elements: is this 'high' or 'low' comedy?
12. How are differences between the two characters brought out?
13. From whose point of view is the story told? Do you remain convinced at the end that the 'I' of the story is the author?
14. How is characterization achieved? (Direct description? Effect on others? Dialogue?)

Read carefully the notes below before going on to the story that follows.

TITLE	An Only Child.
TYPE	A Fable.
UNDERLYING IDEAS	People easily misunderstand each other; man needs to prove his abilities to himself; problems of an only child (Orphan).
TIME	The present. Duration: about 18 hours.
SETTING	Kitchen/mountain. Hints of surrounding village. Symbolic and realistic background.
PLOT	Boy – 'delicate' – successfully climbs difficult mountain, despite mother's opinion of him. Abrupt shifts of time.
CHARACTERS	Two. Nagging, hardworking mother. Silent, determined boy. Conflict. Development of characters. Boy and parent brought together after event.

An Only Child

'Good heavens! Where have you been Ronnie? I've been so worried again. You've been away for three whole hours. I really will be glad when these holidays are over. Such a job having to manage alone. You're a delicate boy. I've told you so, many times. That's what Dr Chambers said to me. "He's a delicate boy, Mrs Nashe," he said. And there you go running round the village. When your father was alive ...'

The boy said nothing as he sat down by the kitchen table. His mother's voice droned on. Soon he knew it would rise to a hysterical pitch. Then she would start crying and come and hug him and tell him how much he meant to her. Ronnie looked up at her. Why does she never smile? Perhaps it is all this work. The dishes, cooking, making the beds. The wrinkles on her face have got so deep and made her look so ugly. Since dad died, her hair has turned grey and she is getting fat. Why doesn't she try to understand and be like other mothers?

Ronnie looked out of the window and shut out his mother's words. 'Switching off,' he called it. He was used to thinking to himself against this background of words. Words, words, words. Did they really mean anything? What did the mountain care about words? Imagine being able to see a whole mountain out of your kitchen window! How many kitchen windows had mountains in them, Ronnie wondered.

Now that the sun was setting, the lower slopes became deep purple. It was the moment Ronnie loved best. Soon it would be dark and the whole mountain would become first a shadow and then nothing. The night would take it away and there would be nothing. But the sun would bring it back again in the morning. In the morning. He would try again. This time ...

The morning sun gleamed on the hard brown rocks and on the trees below which completely hid the valley. Ronnie looked up at the over-hanging ledge above him. Down the middle of it ran a deep crack which looked like a streak of lightning which had been turned into stone. This was what the villagers called 'the bad step' which led to the summit. Ronnie had never gone beyond this point.

Now or never, thought Ronnie as he reached up for the jagged piece of rock that jutted out above his head. The rock was firm and Ronnie pulled himself on to it. Then he looked round trying to decide which would be the best way up. Just to the right of him there was a small stone wedged firmly in the crack. He tested it with his foot. As it did not move, he pressed on it with his whole weight. The stone slithered away silently and Ronnie's foot remained firmly wedged in the crack. He clung desperately to the rock, hardly daring to breathe. His hands felt wet and sticky and sweat trickled into his eyes. The ledge shut out the sun. Everything was suddenly cold and dark and the mountain seemed to be pushing him away from the rock-face with all its might. Ronnie rested there motionless for what seemed hours. After he had regained his breath, he pushed his left knee into the crack and freed his foot. Soon, without even realizing how he was doing it, he was clambering up the crack like a mountain goat. He never once dared to look up. Suddenly, the crack became a thread and then disappeared altogether. For the first time, Ronnie raised his head. He could hardly believe it: he had reached the top!

In the bright sunlight, Ronnie trembled uncontrollably but he felt

happy. He sat above the ledge and looked round. Just behind him
he saw the path which led to the village. This was the 'easy' way up. At
least he would not have to climb down that dreadful crack. Below, he
could see the whole village. There was the main street, and yes, there was
his house! What was his mother doing now, he wondered.

Mrs Nashe had just finished sweeping the parlour. I must not get so
anxious, she thought. I must try and be nicer to Ronnie. He doesn't even
speak to me any more. I nag him too much, I know. But he's so delicate.
Still, I can try. I'll just tidy my hair before he comes in.

She was still sitting at her dressing-table when Ronnie arrived. He
broke into a smile when she turned round: she looked so much younger,
so different! It must be her hair, he thought. No, she's put on lipstick!
And she's smiling.

'Had a nice time, dear?' asked Mrs Nashe.

'Yes, I just went for a short walk, mother,' said Ronnie, and he went
up to his mother and kissed her.

Answer these questions:

1. Why can this story be justifiably called a fable?
2. There are two abrupt transitions in the story. How is the reader
   prepared for them?
3. How important is the setting in this story. In what way does it
   differ from that of the previous story?
4. In what way could this plot be said to be less 'ingenious' than the
   one in the first story?
5. Is the plot complex or simple? Why?
6. Do you get the impression that this is not an isolated incident and
   that there is a 'before' and 'after' to the story? Why?
7. What conflict lies at the centre of the story?
8. Are there any instances of 'foreshadowing' in this story? If so, where
   are they to be found?
9. Would you say that the characters 'develop' as the story progresses?
10. How does this story differ in style from the previous one?
11. In what way do the two characters think and act differently?
12. From whose viewpoint is the story told? Discuss any changes of
    viewpoint that occur. Can the author's presence be felt. Where?
13. How is characterization achieved? (Direct description? Effect on
    others? Action? Dialogue?)
14. Are there any instances of 'interior monologue' in this story. If so,
    where?
15. Which of the two stories would you regard as more successful and
    why?

Exercises

Instructions

Write short stories using each of the paragraphs given below. Each paragraph supplies you with a certain amount of information regarding character and plot from which you should construct your plan. The type of story you should write (i.e. 'entertainment' or 'fable') is indicated in brackets, though you may ignore this if you wish. The paragraphs given are not necessarily 'first' or 'last' and may be incorporated into any part of your story.

You should spend up to two hours on each story and the length should be between 600 and 800 words (not including the number of words in the set paragraph). You are advised to divide your time as follows: plan: up to 25 minutes; writing: up to 75 minutes; re-reading and correction: up to 20 minutes. Give each story a title.

1. Graham squeezed into the lift just as the doors were closing – much to the annoyance of the fat lady who had to take a step backwards to make room for him. In doing so, she trod on the toes of the little man behind her and at the same time completely knocked his hat out of shape. The poor man gazed at it despondently and unsuccessfully tried to pat it back into shape while the lady muttered an apology and glared at Graham. There was a second's pause, and the lift began its long descent from the tenth floor. After a time it stopped and everybody waited for the doors to open, but they did not. Graham peered out into the dark lift shaft. All he could see was a blank wall, grey with dust. Then he turned suddenly and announced gaily, 'I say, I think we're stuck between floors!' (*Entertainment*)

2. Time and again he had been tempted to call her unintelligent. But he could not quite bring himself to it. That would be to cast aspersions on his own character. After all, *he* had married her and *he* certainly was not unintelligent. He was in no doubt about that. How then, he reasoned, could he make an unintelligent choice? No, it was not possible. Suddenly his face lit up: illogical! Yes, that was it, she was illogical. Feminine illogicality. That explained everything. The more he thought about it, the more he found the idea curiously comforting. (*Fable*)

3. I closed the door behind me and from that very moment I felt that there was somebody there and that this somebody was very friendly and pleased to see me. This made me feel very happy. Quite light-heartedly I began to unpack my suit-case and prepare for bed. I placed some shirts on the armchair and some books on the bedside table and started arranging my clothes in the small wardrobe by the window. When I went to get my shirts, I found them on the bed with the books on top of them. At first I thought that I was being absent-minded. But since this happened with a number of other objects, I had the impression that

there was a little boy in the room who was playing tricks on me. I spoke to him kindly, said good-night, and went to bed. (*Ghost-story: entertainment*)

4. At the same time I was overwhelmed by the impression that I had been here before. On the wall opposite the door there was a Japanese print of a horse. The picture was slightly crooked and for a moment this irritated me. I felt an impulse to go over at once and straighten it, but I dared not do so. In the corner there was a badly stained, heavy oak table. It was scratched and I went towards it eagerly wondering whether any of the deeply carved initials would suggest anything to me. (*Fable*)

5. Nine men had been specially selected for the task. Months of training and experience had made them experts in jungle warfare and taught them to be alert and ever-ready for the unexpected. Above all, the men had learned how to act as a team so that each one was responsible for the safety of the others. The group had been ordered to locate the exact position of the enemy and return to base within twenty-four hours. Reports on the enemy's whereabouts were untrustworthy, though they were believed to be in the vicinity of the swamp some five miles away at the other side of the jungle. (*Entertainment* or *Fable*)

6. Human beings are imitative creatures. This is especially true when they live in small communities. One or two individuals set a pattern of behaviour and everybody follows without question for fear of being thought an odd man out. Perhaps this will explain the consternation felt by all the inhabitants of Littleville Row one morning last March. The news soon got round that Alf Plumpson of 'Meadows', 14, Littleville Row, had been seen in his garden. What is more (old Norris had been quite clear about this point when he related it to the bewildered husbands at 'The King's Arms' that Saturday night), Plumpson had not just been *standing* in the garden: he had been *digging* it! (*Fable*)

7. 'And now, Jenkins,' said the doctor, 'when you leave this room you will meet a middle-aged lady who is in the company of her daughter. She claims you are her nephew and that you lived with her until you joined the army. If what she says is true, she is the last relation you saw before you lost your memory. Look at her carefully and see whether her face suggests anything to you. Try and be patient this time because she is sure to ask you a lot of questions.' (*Fable*)

8. 'Oh, it's you is it?' I said as I opened the door. 'Just a minute. I'll get my coat.'

I slammed the door behind me and hurried to the car. It started off immediately.

'Tell me,' I said impatiently, 'are you sure it's him? What was he wearing? Not that green corduroy jacket? I bet he was surprised! What did he have to say? Why are you driving so slowly?'

'Don't be so impatient,' said a voice behind me which I did not recognize. (*Entertainment*)

9. 'This photograph has been tampered with,' said the inspector as he handed it back to Finch. It's identical with the one I have, except that the figure of a man you see crouching in the left-hand corner has been superimposed on the original print. It seems to me that, once again, someone has been trying to get us on to a false track.' (*Detective-story: entertainment*)

10. She was late as usual. For nearly three-quarters of an hour he had been standing under the clock pretending, for the benefit of passers-by, that he had only just that moment arrived. He had spent the first quarter of an hour whistling and staring rudely at people who giggled or whispered as they passed him. He had studied the contents of the shop-window behind him so well, that he knew by heart exactly where everything was. There was a big cream cake in the centre surrounded by a motley assortment of buns and biscuits. Behind that, there was a cardboard figure of a man in a red peak cap holding a tray of what looked like sweets. The figure was grinning hideously and the crumpled white balloon projecting from his parted lips said, 'Why don't you try one?' For what must have been the hundredth time he jerked his sleeve back to look at his watch, as if he was really interested in finding out the time. (*Entertainment* or *Fable*).

11. Now that in the morning it was covered with snow, the square looked like a great white page waiting for the imprint of future footsteps. The writing of the past – the torn autumn leaves, the marks of countless hurrying feet had been washed away. For a short time, the silent, secret snow would remain there like the first page of a diary on which would be recorded the countless impressions of the day. (*Fable*)

12. A guard opened the small prison door and the man emerged. After the door closed behind him, the man stood quite still and looked at the empty street. It was early morning and he breathed deeply. Five years in prison had been a long time. He glanced up at the sky, blinking, like a blind man who has been shown it for the first time. The coarse, cheap material of his new clothes felt strange and unfamiliar. He put his hands into his pockets and gripped the few notes and coins that were there. Then, as if he had suddenly made up his mind about something, he walked briskly down the street. (*Entertainment* or *Fable*)

13. The shout penetrated my sleep, but I soon made it part of my dream. It fitted perfectly into the odd sequence of events which at that moment seemed to be passing before my eyes. The galloping horse had stopped, reared on its hind legs, and instead of whinnying had shouted.

But now the shout rang out louder than before. This time it was impossible to deceive myself about it. I sat up in bed with a start. After a few seconds had passed I dimly realized that someone was shouting in the street. (*Entertainment* or *Fable*)

14. I was brought before a person who, judging from the behaviour of the two creatures that escorted me, seemed to be in a position of authority. His skin was of a different colour from that of my escorts and I at once took this to mean that he belonged to a higher order. Since my capture, I had only seen two other creatures with skin which was that particular shade of blue. Once more, my escorts indicated that I should empty my pockets for the benefit of this superior being. With a sigh, I fished out my handkerchief, cigarettes, lighter, fountain-pen, keys, and other oddments and placed them before him. The only thing that seemed to intrigue him was the cigarettes, and from his gestures I understood that he wanted me to explain what they were. This, I thought, would be a good opportunity for me to illustrate some of my extraordinary powers. I put a cigarette into my mouth and lit it. I gazed at the superior being as I blew a jet of smoke from my mouth and nostrils. This had a very strange effect on him. As far as I could judge, he seemed to be filled with alarm. (*Science-fiction: entertainment*)

15. There is something almost perverse about the curiosity we display when we want to learn what other people think of us. When Geoffrey Tewson had been appointed to the position of private secretary, he knew he would have access to the confidential files of all the employees in the firm. His first action as private secretary was one that he later deeply regretted. On the pretence of having to work overtime ('to get the hang of things' as he explained to Mr Clapforth), he unlocked the big metal cabinet in the director's office when everyone had gone home. It did not take him long to find his own file. With trembling hands he drew out the pink report-card marked T/4703 Tewson, G. H. (*Fable*)

16. Before the end of the funeral service, he began to feel uncomfortable. He looked at all the solemn faces around him and for an instant caught Crabbe's eye. Crabbe gave him a slow, deliberate wink. It was this that started it. From that moment, he was filled with an irresistible desire to burst out laughing. (*Fable* or *Entertainment*)

17. She had always attributed her capacity for telling lies to what she liked to think of as 'an exceptional imagination'. In time, she came to believe that any lie, even a big one, was infinitely preferable to the truth. (*Fable*)

18. 'How would you like to go to a party?' asked Selwyn suddenly. Before I had time to reply, he thrust an invitation-card into my hands and continued, 'This was sent to me by a certain Mr Andrew Addison whom I've never met. From what I hear he's invited a huge number of famous writers and painters and by some accident I was included. Don't

look so worried. This Addison chap's never met me. All you have to
do is to present yourself and say you're Selwyn Grimes, the painter. I'm
sure Addison will be delighted to see you. He might even ask you to paint
his portrait!' (*Entertainment*)

19. I soon realized that the two strangers opposite me in the compart-
ment were talking about me. It had apparently never entered their minds
that I might be able to understand their language for they talked so
loudly that it was possible for me to listen to their conversation without
so much as raising my eyes from the book I was reading. (*Fable*)

20. Miss Corry was one of those people who somehow inspired confidence in anyone who met her. Even complete strangers had been known
to come to her for advice – advice which she was often unwilling to give.
She had listened patiently while Granger had told her about the
difficulties he was in: how he had been accused of embezzlement, how
someone else must have changed the figures in the account books, how
trustworthy he was in every respect. She never suspected for a moment
that the few words she had said to him at the time would have involved
her so deeply in this unpleasant affair. (*Fable* or *Entertainment*)

Fifty ideas for short stories

Instructions

Write short stories of between 600 and 800 words on each of the subjects
given below. Before making notes on character and plot, you should
decide clearly on the *type* of story you wish to write.

Do not spend more than two hours on each story. The best way to
divide your time is as follows: planning: up to 25 minutes; writing: up to
75 minutes; re-reading and correction: up to 20 minutes. Give each story
a title.

1. An athlete suddenly realizes that he has passed his peak as a runner.
   Write a story showing how this has a profound effect on him.
2. A story from the point of view of a deaf-mute who expresses himself
   in writing for the first time in his life.
3. A science fiction story which deals with a 'Cinderella-type' human
   predicament. A man has been given an injection which 'puts him to
   sleep' for two hundred years. When the time is up, he is permitted to
   stay awake for three days only. Then he must return to his 'cell'
   and be re-injected if he wishes to sleep for another two hundred
   years. Describe his efforts to get back to his 'cell' on time.
4. A rich and successful business-man who has everything he could
   want in life buys a remote island and decides to go and live there with
   four carefully selected companions. Write a story describing the
   efforts of these people to find an ideal way of life.

5. A story about a teacher, who as he (or she) gets older, becomes petty-minded and spiteful in his (or her) dealings with young people.

6. You are probably familiar with the story of Faust and Mephistopheles. Write an amusing story in a modern setting in which Mephistopheles pays a vist to Faust with the object of winning him over. Faust's ideas of hell, based on his experiences of the modern world, are far more frightening than the devil's old-fashioned notions. In the end, Mephistopheles is forced to flee in terror.

7. Write a short opening chapter to a novel called 'The Cage'

8. Two ex-fighter pilots return to civilian life. After the excitements of war, they find it very difficult to settle down to dull, steady jobs. Write a story showing how their desire for excitement and violence makes them turn to crime.

9. Six old men meet regularly in a park and spend the day together. One day one of them dies and this is followed shortly afterwards by the death of another. The knowledge that one of the remaining four will be next has a peculiar effect on them and leads to curious speculations.

10. Put yourself in the position of a long-distance cyclist. Write an 'interior monologue' describing what goes on in your mind during a particularly arduous race.

11. An amusing story about a person who is obsessed by the idea that he must give up smoking. All his efforts are in vain, for every time he stops smoking, he always finds a good reason which justifies his starting again.

12. A young person who has lived all his life in Africa has long dreamed of visiting the country from which his parents had once emigrated. In his mind, he has built up a fanciful idea of this country and its people. Write a story showing how he is sadly disillusioned when he at last visits his country of origin.

13. An amusing story about an innocent-looking, charming old lady who outwits a gang of formidable thieves.

14. A famous writer is reported killed while hunting big game. The next day he has the dubious pleasure of reading his obituary in a morning newspaper. Imagine his reactions and how he writes a reply to the astonished Editor.

15. A horror story about a ventriloquist's doll.

16. A story satirizing 'red tape'

17. A story about an extremely conventional person who has the idea that he leads a wildly unconventional life.

18. An amusing story called 'The New Maid'.

19. A story about a person who, when young, was regarded by everyone as a man of promise but is now a miserable failure.

20. A story about an unimaginative and stubborn missionary who arouses the hostility of the tribe he has come to convert.

21. The story of Hansel and Gretel in an entirely modern setting (e.g. the witch could be a 'nice' old lady in a sweet shop).

22. A story about a once-respected judge who ends up as a criminal. He is brought to trial and is judged by a man whom he had once sentenced to prison.

23. An amusing story describing the unpleasantness of having workmen in the house.

24. A story called 'The Tooth-ache'.

25. A story about a person who is too proud to apologize even when he is in the wrong.

26. A story about a man whose doctor has given him three months to live.

27. Four men have planned a perfect escape from a prison. Two days before their attempt a new prisoner is put into the same cell. The prisoners are obliged to take him into their confidence. The new prisoner takes an active part in the preparations that are being made but at the last moment he betrays his fellow-inmates.

28. A story about a man who, while on a journey to a distant town, decides to look up an old friend whom he has not seen since his school-days. After all these years the friend has changed very much and he pretends that he does not recognize his visitor. In the end, the man leaves not sure whether his old friend has recognized him or not.

29. Two prisoners who are bitter enemies have been handcuffed together and are being transferred to a different prison by truck. During the journey they escape. Give an account of their efforts to be free of each other.

30. Write the last chapter of a novel entitled 'The Angry Young Woman'.

31. A story illustrating the idea that one can feel extremely lonely when living in a big city.

32. A story bringing out the relationship between a father and his son. The father is the head of a large and flourishing company and he wants his son to follow his footsteps. The son, however, wishes to become a musician.

33. A ghost-story about an old family portrait which is said to have the power to hypnotize anyone who looks at it for too long.

34. A Victorian children's story (with a moral) about a little boy who was *too* good. Begin 'Once upon a time ...' Imagine that you are addressing two young listeners who interrupt you occasionally.

35. A story about a man who closely resembles a famous actor and is, as a result, pestered by unknown people for autographs etc. This has such an effect on his character that in the end he comes to believe that he *is* the famous actor.

36. A story about a circus clown who is getting old and tired. Imagine what goes on in his mind as he entertains his audience.
37. A story about two tramps discussing what they might have become and concluding that they are better off as they are.
38. A story about a medium who is a fraud.
39. A story set in any period in the past in which you imagine an entirely fictitious episode in the life of a famous historical character.
40. An amusing story about a young man who discovers to his horror that he is going bald and tries in vain to save his hair.
41. A detective story about a valuable picture which is stolen from an art gallery.
42. A story about a factory worker who refuses to take part in a strike.
43. An elderly man (or woman) accidentally finds three or four letters which he received in his youth and which throw light on an event he (or she) had completely forgotten.
44. A science-fiction horror story. Imagine a world in which scientists have found the secret of immortality, but with one important distinction: people cannot die (except by accident) but they become more and more senile.
45. A story entirely in dialogue about a husband and wife who have decided to separate.
46. The final pages of a journal kept by an explorer who died before he managed to reach his destination.
47. A man who is presumed to have been killed in battle returns home two years after the war is over. Give an account of what happens after his arrival.
48. The 'interior monologue' of a mad but very imaginative boy.
49. A story about a small grocer who is forced out of business by two big rival concerns against which he cannot compete.
50. A story about a respectable doctor with an appalling past. His position is threatened by someone who attempts to blackmail him.

The reflective essay

Instructions
A reflective essay is an exercise in contemplation on any given subject.
It tests your ability to think and describe, to order your ideas and to draw
on your experience, imagination, and general knowledge.

1. TYPES Though reflective essays cannot be easily classified, there are,
by and large, two distinct groups: those which require a great deal of
description as well as reflection which we may call 'descriptive-reflective'; and those in which the emphasis is on reasoning rather than
description which we may call 'abstract'.

(a) *Descriptive-reflective* These usually take the form of one-word titles.
When writing you should draw conclusions from what you describe.
'Gardening,' for instance, is a title of this sort. Here you would not only
be expected to describe gardening but to express your views on it.

(b) *Abstract* These again may take the form of one-word titles when they
refer to abstract qualities (i.e. 'Truth'). Very often, however, the title
appears as a phrase beginning with the word 'On' (e.g. 'On having to
work'). In subjects of this kind, purely descriptive writing is of secondary importance. Your ability to reason rather than to describe, your
own feelings and views about the subject take first place.

2. INTERPRETING THE SUBJECT It is extremely important for you to
understand what is required by the subject before you begin planning
your essay. A reflective essay title may often have a wide number of
implications so that it is possible to interpret it in a variety of ways.
Consider, for example, a subject like 'Walls'. If you interpreted this as a
'descriptive-reflective' title, in your essay you would describe actual
walls and express your feelings about them. Here are a few ideas which
might be included in an approach of this sort: the walls of your own
room or house; those surrounding buildings, gardens etc.; interior and
exterior walls; defensive walls in history; walls in old historic buildings;
ruined walls; walls in fields; walls as seen by a person in a hospital or
prison; defaced walls in cities or in a nursery; decorated walls or blank
walls; walls made of different types of materials etc.

The subject, however, may also be interpreted metaphorically as an 'abstract' one. For instance, walls could be taken to be hurdles in life providing man with a challenge; conversely, they could be seen as things which impede man, which isolate him and prevent him from loving his neighbour in that they exist between houses and between countries as political barriers; mountain ranges, rivers, frontiers, and different languages are 'walls'; or you could confine yourself to a consideration of *why* man builds walls at all: are they the result of suspicion, the desire to protect himself, the desire for privacy?

Once you have *interpreted* a subject in this way, you are ready to begin planning your essay. You may deal with a great number of points or limit yourself to a consideration of just one or two. But you must *never* confuse a 'descriptive-reflective' approach with an 'abstract' one. In the subject given above, for instance, it would be absurd to deal with walls in a nursery in one paragraph and with the metaphorical 'walls' which divide nations in the next. Keep to *one* approach.

3. SUBJECT-MATTER What you have to say is quite as important as how you say it. An essay may be well written and well organized but still lack *substance*. When this is the case, the fault usually lies in a poor interpretation of the subject. Avoid making trite observations like 'Every time I think about walls' or 'We see walls everywhere' or 'Walls are very useful' etc. Another thing to avoid is what might be called the 'pseudo-historical' approach. This consists in giving the 'history' of the subject from the earliest times to the present. Essays of this sort usually go something like this: 'Many years ago when men were living in caves they did not have walls, but as time went by etc., etc.' Crude writing of this sort can be avoided if the subject is interpreted in a satisfactory way.

4. TREATMENT Two distinct processes are involved in essay-writing: analysis and synthesis. In the first instance, you break down the subject (analysis) and then put it together again (synthesis) so that it forms *a complete whole*. Nothing irrelevant must be included. Your essay should have unity to the extent that if any single part were excluded it would spoil the effect of the whole. Like a painting or a piece of music, an essay is a *composition*. When complete, it should not be possible to add or subtract anything.

Your work must be balanced and well proportioned. You can only achieve this if you fully understand the purpose of the paragraph. Each paragraph in your essay is a unit of thought which deals with an aspect of the main theme. In the same way, each sentence must contribute something to the central thought of each paragraph. If an essay can be defined as a group of related paragraphs, a paragraph can be defined as a group of related sentences.

Transitions from one paragraph to another should be smooth. A paragraph may often warn the reader of the approach of a new thought or refer to an idea that has already been considered. Each paragraph should be developed properly: a sentence or two is not enough. From the point of view of the reader, a paragraph is a logical break which allows him to collect his thoughts, as much as it is a physical break which permits him to rest his eyes.

The function of the *Introduction*, *Development*, and *Conclusion* is as follows:

(a) *Introduction* This is the most important paragraph in the essay as it is here that you make clear to the reader your interpretation of the subject. An introduction is, in effect, an essay in miniature, for you should touch briefly on some of the main aspects of the subject. In other words, your introduction should lead the reader to expect certain things.

(b) *Development* In this part of the essay you should take up the points that were hinted at in the introduction. Each main point must be developed fully in a single paragraph and all the paragraphs should be related to each other in some way. Avoid 'listing', that is, beginning paragraphs with phrases like 'The first thing we must consider ...', 'The second point ...' etc. Your essay should be well-constructed, but your plan should not 'come through' your work. The fact that you have planned your essay should on no account be obvious to the reader.

(c) *Conclusion* This should in some way relate to the introduction and so round the essay off. Do not end abruptly. At the same time, avoid clumsy phrases like, 'To sum up ...' or 'Thus we see ...' etc.

5. DEVICES: *Description, Illustration, Contrast.*

(a) *Description* This will form an important part of your essays as in 'descriptive-reflective' topics (as the title implies) and even occasionally in 'abstract' ones, your comments will be based largely on what you describe. You may draw on your experience when dealing with subjects that are familiar to you (say, 'Photography') or on your imagination and general knowledge when writing about less familiar topics (say, 'Mirages').

(b) *Illustration* Do not make comments without being able to prove them by giving examples. Illustration is especially important when you are dealing with 'abstract' topics. If, for instance, you are writing about a subject like 'Fear', good examples will make your meaning immediately clear to the reader.

(c) *Contrast* This gives variety to your writing and makes what you have to say more interesting. If in one paragraph you have given one view of a subject, it is often wise to deal with a completely opposite view in the next. This has the effect of surprising the reader and enabling him to see the subject in a new light.

6. HUMOUR A light approach is often highly suitable in reflective essays. You may poke fun at certain beliefs and activities in a way that will not only amuse your reader but also give him an unusual point of view. Irony, satire, and even parody (imitating the style of someone else in such a way as to ridicule it) are frequently the necessary elements of a light essay. Let us say you hate gardening. You can convey your dislike by observing ironically that it is enjoyable to do hard work, to get wet and muddy, to plant things that never grow, etc.

7. STYLE

(a) *Suitability* The style you adopt for each essay must match your approach to the subject. Irony, for instance, would be quite out of place in an essay on photography in which you have made it your aim to deal with some of the technical aspects of the subject. Similarly, it is not possible to 'switch' from a serious consideration of a topic to a humorous one unless there is a very special reason.

(b) *Personal and Impersonal* Unless you are *specifically* asked to give your views on the subject, do not write in the first person as the capital 'I' is likely to figure prominently in your essay. When writing in the third person, avoid making vague or pompous generalizations (e.g. 'Everybody realizes how important it is to travel ...' etc.). Or this sort of false modesty: 'In our humble opinion ...' etc.

(c) *Use of Words* The key to good writing is simplicity. Do not write long, involved sentences or use a long word where a short one will do. It is important to realize that your writing will be simple and clear when, and only when, you have something definite to say and know what you are talking about.

8. PLANNING Like a sound building, a well-constructed essay requires a full and detailed plan. You may in the course of writing depart from it, but this should be the exception rather than the rule.

A good way to make out a plan is as follows: Leave a wide margin on the left-hand side of the page. In the left-hand column, note your ideas in any order as they occur to you. These notes will provide you with the raw material for your plan which should be written out on the right. Each paragraph-outline on the right should consist of a central thought and a few subsidiary ideas related to it. As you become more and more proficient, it will become less and less necessary to make out a very detailed plan.

Examine carefully the plan below and note its relation to the essay that follows.

TITLE Tourists.

TYPE Descriptive-reflective.

INTERPRETATION Tourism today is a highly organized affair. The average tourist sees very little of the country he visits.

IDEAS	PLAN
Pamphlets etc.	*Introduction*
Planning the holiday.	1. World a small place: the past (Marco
Tourist at home.	Polo) – pamphlets &c. Travel agencies.
Winter.	*Development*
Calculations.	2. Planning the holiday: the tourist at
Post-cards.	home – winter – decisions to be made.
Marco-Polo.	Calculations.
Local colour.	3. Effect on friends – work – postcards.
Souvenirs.	Holiday a comfort during winter months.
Ruins, resorts.	4. Time approaching – countries getting
Beaches.	ready: ruins, resorts – typical scenes–
Countries: typical scenes.	local colour. Welcome. Souvenirs.
Rush. Fortnight's	5. Arduous sight-seeing. Sees little.
holiday.	Post-cards home.
Travel agencies.	*Conclusion*
Programmes: sees little.	6. Fortnight over. Returns 'refreshed'.
Back to work.	Another year's work ahead.

Tourists

By coach, by train, by ship, and by plane, millions of tourists annually depart from home like migrating summer birds. They provide the best possible evidence to prove that the world is not nearly as big as it used to be. For the modern tourist is no Marco Polo. He ventures forth into the unknown and returns home in a matter of weeks, not years. Furthermore, he is armed with pamphlets, maps, and weighty guide-books which tell him where to go and how to get there; and where to stay, what to see and what to eat when he arrives. There are travel agencies everywhere to cater for his needs and make all the necessary preparations for him. They make out ambitious programmes and promise to whisk him through as many as six countries in fourteen days or, if he is in a hurry, they will cover much the same ground in eight or less.

The tourist begins planning his campaign in the dismal winter months. Spread out before him on the floor is a splendid array of brightly-coloured leaflets all of them equally tempting. Now is the time for big decisions to be made, for a fortnight's holiday is not to be squandered lightly. Would he like to ski in the morning and swim in the afternoon? Would he like to go to a place where the sun shines *all the year round*? Would he like to taste the rare delicacies of a distant seaside restaurant? And above all, would he like to visit a spot where there are *no other tourists*? It is all there for the asking. Shivering before the fire and armed with paper and pencil, the tourist makes rapid calculations. It takes him a long time to decide in which particular paradise he should invest his hard-earned money.

Once he has made up his mind, the tourist is free from worry. He now has something definite to discuss with his friends at the office. They listen with envy as he talks knowledgeably about a stretch of coastline which is two thousand miles away. These poor old stay-at-homes wonder how he came to be so well informed and beg him to send them post-cards. In the tourist's mind there is now a little haven of peace and quiet which he can retire to when life gets too much for him. The idea that he will visit a place where the inhabitants do not know what an overcoat is, consoles and comforts him during the bitter winter months.

Winter passes and the time draws near. The simple tourist is often innocent of the fact that most countries in the world have become tourist-conscious. For months now, each country has been advertising its beaches and cities, its ruins and resorts, in a frantic endeavour to make ends meet. It does its best to measure up to the tourist's pre-conceived notions of what he will find on arrival. So it goes out of its way to provide him with 'typical' scenes: that is 'typical' peasants in 'typical' costumes, and customs that should have fallen into decay long ago, but have been given a new lease of life to add to local colour. Representatives of the tourist organization give the traveller a hearty welcome the moment he arrives, and the vendors of trinkets and souvenirs do a brisk trade.

It is small wonder that the tourist is a busy man. He no sooner sets foot on foreign soil than he is rushed to his hotel and thence is immediately taken on a conducted tour of the city by night. In the morning, he goes through another arduous course of sight-seeing. He has barely had the chance to recover, or indeed, to find out exactly where his hotel is located, before he is off again to yet another part of the country. It is not even a bird's eye view he gets. Rather, it is a snap-shot view.

He is given about half an hour on each famous site and has just about enough time to take photographs which he can sort out when he gets home. In the perpetual race against time, he is forever sending postcards to his friends depicting wonderful views of places he never knew existed, let alone saw.

No fortnight in the year passed quite so quickly. Travel-worn, the tourist eventually arrives home proudly displaying his collection of passport-stamps. Truly rested, he is back at the office on Monday with a year's work ahead of him before he will have the opportunity to sally forth again.

Answer these questions:

1. Why can this essay be justifiably called 'descriptive-reflective'?
2. What other interpretations of the subject can you think of in addition to that given by the writer?
3. Does the writer stick to one approach throughout the essay? If so, how?
4. Comment on the subject matter (e.g. Does the essay *say* anything worth saying? Are any of the statements made obvious or trite?).
5. Could any paragraph be cut out without affecting the unity of the essay?
6. Is the essay well-balanced and proportioned? Are the transitions from one paragraph to another smooth?
7. To what extent could the introduction be called an 'essay in miniature'? Does it contain the writer's interpretation of the subject?
8. Do the succeeding paragraphs *develop* the subject? How?
9. Is the conclusion appropriate? Why?
10. Pick out descriptive passages and comment on their function.
11. What use – if any — is made of illustration?
12. Is there any contrast in this essay? If so, give examples.
13. Is the approach serious or light? Justify your answer.
14. What use is made of irony and parody?
15. Does the style of writing match the writer's approach to the subject?
16. Can you see any positive advantages in the use of the third person? Which?
17. Comment on the writer's use of words (e.g. Is the writing simple and clear? Are there any striking phrases? etc.).
18. Why is a full plan necessary for an essay of this sort?

Examine carefully the plan below and then note its relation to the essay that follows.

TITLE Tradition.
TYPE Abstract.
INTERPRETATION Tradition is not a fixed thing: it changes slowly but surely.

IDEAS	PLAN
Accepting the new:	*Introduction*
a struggle.	1. Word misunderstood: how? – Not
Lasting value?	personally involved – tradition a fixed
'Revaluations':	thing: mistaken. Why?
institutions and beliefs.	*Development*
Misunderstood.	2. Acceptance of the new: a struggle:
War.	testing-ground for ideas.
Darwin.	3. Expand above para. Novelty attractive
What is tradition?	on surface: women's fashions; 'revaluation'
Ever-changing.	of arts, politics etc. Value?
Social revolution:	4. Exception: e.g. atomic energy.
dramatic changes:	Dramatic changes. Process slow: e.g.
atomic energy.	social revolution.
Slow assimilation.	5. How new ideas are accepted: half
Harmony – music.	accepted by one generation; completely
Sensibility.	by next. Why? Widening sensibility:
City.	e.g. Darwin, music: withstood test.
Ancestors and successors.	*Conclusion*
Testing-ground.	6. Like a city: always changing:
	ancestors and successors.

Tradition

Because the word 'tradition' is used loosely, it is frequently misunderstood. It is often associated with actions and beliefs which do not involve us personally; which persist for no better reason than that they are 'traditional'. It is regarded as a fixed thing, rigidly hostile to change, to be defended against those who threaten to overthrow it. Nothing could be more mistaken. Tradition is not only made up of our important beliefs, but the great host of trivial daily habits and customs we acquire in the course of growing up. Nor is it inflexible. New ideas are continually being adapted to fit in with the old. The process is slow but sure. And when old ideas become so outmoded that they no longer serve their purpose, they are discarded.

The acceptance of new ideas always involves a struggle; people do not easily give up notions they hold dear. In this way, tradition protects itself, for by providing a testing-ground for the new, it allows only what is of some value to assert itself.

This is how tradition acts as a safeguard against the easy acceptance of new ideas which seem to be attractive on the surface. It is never possible for us to decide whether a new scheme will be of lasting value or not. What seem to be startlingly new and exciting trends in the arts or in politics or in science after a few years can often be seen to have amounted to very little. The desire for novelty which is of such importance in women's fashions or car design sometimes affects our most important beliefs and institutions. We are often urged by the press and in books to 're-value' or to 're-examine' long-established views which have taken centuries to form and to replace them by opinions which have been concocted in a few hours or weeks. How many such 'revaluations', one wonders, will be remembered in a few year's time?

It is true that sometimes a discovery is made which completely alters our outlook. Ideas which have been held for centuries can occasionally be swept away over-night. In our own times, for instance, advances in nuclear physics have totally changed our 'traditional' conception of warfare. The very word 'war' has now taken on a new meaning which was unknown as recently as 1944. Dramatic changes of this sort, however, are unusual. The big social revolution we have witnessed in the twentieth century still has a long way to go before reaching anything like perfection.

Ideas which are half-accepted by one generation, are often completely accepted by the one that follows. Innovations are bitterly attacked by those who cannot conceive of a new order and are judged by standards of the past. This is because people's sensibilities are confined to what they have always known and believed. What was new to one generation is easily assimilated by another because sensibility has widened sufficiently to allow a notion that was once considered radical or extreme to establish itself. A good example of this is the publication of *The Origin of Species* in 1859. The prolonged and bitter controversy which Darwin's work provoked has lingered down to this day. But whereas, initially, Darwin's arguments were hotly disputed, they have since become part of our cultural heritage. That is to say, they no longer shock our sensibilities. In the same way, modern music, for instance, does not strike us as discordant because it does not conform with former conceptions of harmony. What were once new ideas have withstood the test tradition has imposed on them.

Our view of the past is forever changing. Tradition is like a great city which is growing all the time. Old buildings are demolished and new ones put up. Each new building, however large or small, alters our view of the shape and size of existing ones. The city we look upon is not the one our ancestors saw; nor is it the one we shall hand down to our successors.

Answer these questions:

1. Why can this essay be justifiably called 'abstract'? How does it differ from the previous one?
2. What other interpretations of the subject can you think of in addition to that given by the writer?
3. Does the writer stick to one approach throughout the essay? if so, how?
4. Comment on the subject-matter (e.g. Does the essay *say* anything worth saying? Are any of the statements made obvious or trite?)
5. Could any paragraph be cut out without affecting the unity of the essay?
6. Is the essay well-balanced and proportioned? Are the transitions from one paragraph to another smooth?
7. To what extent could the introduction be called an 'essay in miniature'? Does it contain the writer's interpretation of the subject?
8. Do the succeeding paragraphs *develop* the subject? How?
9. Is the conclusion appropriate? Why?
10. Why are there no descriptive passages in this essay?
11. What use is made of illustration? Comment on (a) its suitability (b) its function.
12. Is there any contrast in this essay? If so, give examples.
13. Is the approach serious or light? Justify your answer.
14. How does the writer's approach in this essay differ from the previous one? Would it have been possible to treat a subject like this lightly?
15. Does the style of writing match the writer's approach to the subject?
16. Comment on the writer's use of words. Why is this essay 'more difficult' than the previous one?
17. Why is a full plan necessary for an essay of this sort?

Preliminary exercises

Instructions

Write essays based on the five detailed plans given below. You may depart from the set plans in places if you wish. The length of each essay should be between 600 and 800 words. You should spend about an hour and a half on each essay (up to 70 minutes writing; up to 20 minutes re-reading and correcting).

1.   TITLE **The Sea.**
         TYPE **Descriptive-reflective.**
INTERPRETATION **People have different attitudes according to circumstances.**

IDEAS	PLAN
Travel.	*Introduction*
Immensity.	1. Immensity: Pacific Ocean seen from
Columbus.	outer space: hardly any land at all: only
Watery planet.	Tahiti visible. A watery planet. Man's
Those inland/islanders.	attitude to sea depends on circumstances.
Cousteau.	*Development*
Bathyscaphe.	2. Attitude in the past: fear of the
Russian plain.	unknown – Columbus – the edge of the
Holidays.	world. Attitude in the present: in a sense,
Science.	sea no less mysterious; man has much to
Life.	learn.
Minerals.	3. Attitude of people who live close to sea,
Food.	islanders etc. – familiarity but respect –
Water.	source of food. Attitude of those living
World population.	far inland (e.g. Russian plains): sea a
The future.	complete mystery.
	4. For the average person: pleasure:
	holiday-makers – beaches – sunshine –
	travel – ocean-going liners.
	5. For the scientist: source of life: study
	of sea-life; variety. Possible source of
	minerals; food for growing world
	population: plankton. Freshwater supply
	(e.g. Kuwait).
	Conclusion
	6. Sea as a challenge: has always been –
	now more than ever. Undersea
	exploration: new methods – Cousteau –
	depth: bathyscaphe etc. Regardless of
	attitude: perhaps it contains the answers
	to some of our biggest problems.

4

2.   TITLE On having an inferiority complex.
                TYPE Abstract.
INTERPRETATION Humorous approach. 'Anything I can do you can do
                better.'

IDEAS	PLAN
Psychologists.	*Introduction*
'Complex'.	1. Amusing account of the term
Comparing ourselves	'complex': inferiority, superiority,
with others.	Oedipus – fashionable to have one.
Superior people.	Psychologists thrive on them. But not a
The Joneses.	modern phenomenon: complexes existed
Material possessions.	before psychologists.
Space-race.	*Development*
Fashionable.	2. The individual: who hasn't got one?
The family.	Why? Those with superiority complexes
Babies.	are few but they are dynamic,
Tyrants.	domineering, aggressive. They rule the
Comparisons.	world. Better than us at everything. We
Bombs.	eat too much, sleep too much, blush too
Who is to blame?	much, while they …
	3. Where does it begin? The nursery:
	younger brothers and sisters so much
	better than we are: know how to hold a
	knife and fork, how to behave etc. Babies
	(little tyrants) rule the world, make *us*
	feel *small*!
	4. Collective inferiority complex: the
	family; keeping up with the Joneses:
	material possessions – cars, TV etc.
	Father just not good enough.
	5. National inferiority complex: affects
	even the most progressive nations: e.g.
	space-race. Lesser nations also want 'the
	bomb'. Complex measured in terms of
	size of bomb: the smaller the bomb, the
	bigger the complex.
	Conclusion
	6. Psychologists are really to blame: if
	they had not invented the term we would
	have gone on having complexes and have
	been none the wiser.

3.   TITLE Faces.
            TYPE Descriptive-reflective.
INTERPRETATION Immense variety.

IDEAS	PLAN
Variety.	*Introduction*
Twins.	1. The most striking and memorable
Crowds.	thing about any individual. Why? Face
Expression.	betrays personality, emotions. All faces
Beauty/Ugliness.	have same simple components, yet
Youth/Age.	infinite variety.
Cleopatra, Helen of	*Development*
Troy.	2. Exception: twins: delight us because
Gargoyles, clowns, giants.	they do not conform.
Photographs.	3. Impression of variety: crowds (e.g. a
Portraits.	football match, a railway station). We
Loved ones.	get blurred impressions. We remember
Telephones.	emotions expressed but not particular
Radios.	faces.
Football matches.	4. Variety of youth and age. Course of
	human life traced on the face: details:
	eyes, mouth, hair, etc. Human face is
	expressive regardless of age.
	5. Beauty and ugliness only relative.
	No such thing as perfect beauty or
	absolute ugliness. Transformed by our
	imagination: e.g. Cleopatra, Helen of
	Troy. Ugliest faces the same: e.g.
	gargoyles, giants. Amusing distortions:
	circus clowns.
	6. Faces of loved ones. Hard to remember
	when they are away. Thus: photographs,
	portraits and delights they afford. What
	we remember is certain expressions: ways
	of looking, laughing, etc.
	Conclusion
	7. Impossible to imagine 'faceless'
	human beings. Tendency to 'invent'
	faces to fit voices heard on radio,
	telephone, etc. Why? Because when we
	think of a person, we think of a face.

4.   TITLE Greatness.
      TYPE Abstract.
INTERPRETATION Ordinary men and women are capable of greatness.

IDEAS	PLAN
What we mean.	*Introduction*
Achievement.	1. What we first think of when we hear
Names: de Vinci	the phrase 'great men and women':
Shakespeare	achievement. Our custom to measure
Napoleon	'greatness' solely in terms of
Rimbaud	achievement: perhaps mistaken because
Goethe	judged by a different set of values
Fleming	ordinary men and women could be 'great'.
Pasteur etc.	*Development*
Benefactors.	2. Achievement: History and the Arts.
Great life: what is it?	Great names (e.g. Thucydides,
Define.	Charlemagne, Magellan, Beethoven,
Ordinary people.	Shakespeare, da Vinci, etc.). Great, not
Great people but not	for themselves as individuals, but for
great lives.	what they did.
	3. Same true of benefactors: Pasteur,
	Fleming, Koch, the Curies. Not their
	lives we remember but their achievements.
	4. Great people do not necessarily lead
	'great' lives: e.g. Milton, Napoleon,
	Rimbaud, etc.
	5. What is a 'great life'? Define the full
	and 'good' life: enjoyment of work and
	play; qualities of tolerance, consideration,
	understanding, zest, peace of mind, etc.
	Difficult to achieve because it requires deep
	understanding of oneself and one's place
	in the world: 'the unexamined life is not
	worth living' (Socrates).
	Conclusion
	6. Seen in these terms, it is possible for
	certain ordinary men and women to lead
	'great' lives. They will not be
	remembered for their achievements but
	that makes them no less great.

5.   TITLE Men and Machines.

          TYPE Descriptive-reflective.

INTERPRETATION Semi-humorous approach: who rules the world: men or machines?

IDEAS	PLAN
Labour-saving devices. Telephones, refrigerators etc. Big machines. Power plants. Los Angeles. Transistor radios: noise everywhere. Computors. 'Clever' machines. Wooden machines: the past. Drudgery. Automation. Science fiction. Who's boss? Machines that make machines.	*Introduction* 1. Machines as the expression of man's desire to be relieved from drudgery. From early efforts: clumsy wooden contraptions to electrical computors. Have they done away with drudgery or just made more? *Development* 2. In the home: labour-saving devices. Gadgets that go wrong: boilers, washing machines, refrigerators, telephones, etc. They serve us but how long do we spend looking after them? 3. Colossal machines that make or control other machines: power-houses, atomic energy stations, hydro-electric plants. Size of man by comparison. What happens when they go wrong: chaos: power-cuts, communications, factories. Disposal of atomic waste. 4. Some effects on man: the invasion of the world by machines: cars, pneumatic drills. The countryside: transistors. Noise. Some cities designed more for machines than for men: e.g. Los Angeles: huge car parks. 5. Sophisticated machines: electrical computors, teaching machines. Science-fiction fantasy: will they grow so clever that they will drive us out altogether? *Conclusion* 6. Man's dream: complete automation: Utopia. Leisure. If that time really comes, who will then rule the world?

Exercises

Instructions

Write essays using each of the paragraphs given below. Each paragraph supplies you with a certain amount of information about the subject. Using this as a starting-point, you should construct a full and detailed plan of your own. These paragraphs are not necessarily 'first' or 'last'. You will be able to see how they fit into the general scheme only after you have made your plan. The title of each essay is given in brackets.

You should spend up to two hours on each essay and the length should be between 600 and 800 words (not including the number of words in the set paragraphs). You are advised to divide your time as follows: planning: up to 25 minutes; writing: up to 75 minutes; re-reading and correction: up to 20 minutes.

1. The cultivation of a hobby not only allows us to relax properly, but it gives us a true sense of proportion. People in quite minor positions, as well as those who have many responsibilities to bear, often have an exaggerated idea of their own importance and consider themselves to be indispensable. They regard anything unconnected with their work with suspicion and are afraid even to take a holiday. 'Who will take care of things when I'm gone?' they ask, unaware that 'things' will go on just the same when they have really gone for good and there will always be someone else to take care of them. Hobbies redress the balance by helping us to understand how full life is. The man who really works well is he who can completely forget his work in the intervening hours when he is left to himself. (*Hobbies*)

2. Our passion for erecting huge clocks in public places is only one expression of our slavery to the idea of punctuality. Immense clocks embedded in the towers of town halls and churches frown down on a hurrying populace perpetually reminding them that they must be on time. It is said that the nearer man gets to the equator, the less inclination he has to be punctual. If one can judge from the comparative dearth of public clocks in warm countries, this statement must be true. In these places, the world goes by in a leisurely way: there is no unseen enemy lurking in the background, timing the lives of the inhabitants with a stop-watch. (*On not being punctual*)

3. Islanders are used to living in small, compact communities where self-sufficiency and isolation are valued. The risk of being cut off from the mainland for weeks at a time, is one they are willing to take. They become as much a part of the islands on which they live as the surrounding sea. Just as the wind carves fissures in the rocks, it cuts deep lines in their faces and hardens their features. A stranger, alien to their way of

life, is often viewed with suspicion; but once accepted, friendship is lasting. (*Islands*)

4. Mosquitoes belong to this second group: they go into the attack with no provocation at all. At least they have the decency to warn you of their approach. It is a mystery how so flimsy a creature manages to make so much noise. Turning on the bedside light and facing up to the enemy is no solution. The mosquito has an uncanny sense of impending danger and disappears into thin air as surely as the genie in the fairy story. Your only hope is to dive under the bedclothes and spend the rest of the night gasping for breath. There can hardly be a human being who is not prepared to suffocate to death rather than go through this most unpleasant form of blood-transfusion. (*Insects*)

5. The standard of the Games, too, is extraordinarily high. Records are continually broken as if there were no limit to human endurance and skill. But underlying all this, the essential spirit of the ancient Olympic Games remains. Competitors may still be disqualified for not acting fairly; the prizes they win have a symbolic value only. The modern Games continue to reflect the Greek idea that man must cultivate both physical and mental qualities, and that both the body and mind should be subjected to discipline. (*The Olympic Games*)

6. No self-respecting newspaper these days contents itself with the mere presentation of news. For a very small amount of money each day, we are not simply informed of affairs of national and international importance. We are given photographs of people and places; the famous and notorious unfold their best-kept secrets, side by side with the not-so-famous who, for one reason or another, have 'hit the headlines'. This is not all we get for our money. There is always plenty of advice about what plays or films to see; what books to read; how we should dress; what we should eat; and where we should spend our holidays. And in case we have nothing better to do, we are provided with the most effective of time-killers: quizzes and crossword-puzzles. (*Newspapers*)

7. But fortune-tellers have not really disappeared: they have simply turned professional. Hardly a newspaper or magazine is without one. And what they have to say is always front-page news. 'Your Horoscope' figures prominently side by side with the latest reports on re-armament or dis-armament or the havoc wreaked by a recent hurricane. The fortune-teller of today is presumably a respectable, well-dressed individual who knocks off from work at five o'clock like the rest of us – after, of course, first taking the precaution to lock away his crystal ball in the cupboard. (*On consulting the stars*)

8. Nylon is an extremely tough and durable fibre which has many excellent qualities. Clothing made of nylon does not shrink or lose its

shape; it does not crease easily; and it can withstand far more rubbing, soaking, and rough wear than ordinary fabrics. Nylon not only stands up to water, but to fire as well, for it is not inflammable: it melts but does not burn. Thus, the risk of fire is reduced to a minimum. It has yet another extraordinary characteristic: it repels insects. Moths, which can cause great damage to woollen goods, do not find nylon attractive and leave it alone. (*Nylon*)

9. Witches wielded enormous influence and their methods became well known. They were said to make images of their victims out of wax or wood. The image had a two-fold purpose. If evil was to be brought on the victim, it was mutilated; if he was to be cured of an illness, it could be done without personal attention, simply by tending the image. Witches were also said to cast spells. They would repeat certain phrases and so cause harm to those who had incurred their displeasure. As with wax images, the influence of spells could also be used to bring about health and happiness. Thus many ignorant country people sought the aid of witches to ensure a good harvest. (*Witchcraft*)

10. Day-dreaming is such a universal practice because it requires very little effort. Even while washing the dishes you can retire to your own private little world and identify yourself with your ideal hero. Nobody would ever suspect from the smile on your face that you have not only been washing plates, but successfully demolishing a sea-monster with your bare hands. (*Day-dreams*)

11. Money also acts as a common measure of value. If we had to rely on the barter system, it would be impossible, for instance, to calculate how many loaves of bread we should have to offer our dentist for taking care of our teeth. Furthermore, payment in kind does not allow freedom of choice: the dentist would be obliged to accept far more bread than he could use. Money enables us to buy exactly what we need and acts as a measure for quantity and quality. (*Money*)

12. It is not difficult to understand why an eclipse of the sun or moon instilled terror into the hearts of primitive peoples. Natural phenomena like rain, storms, and the wind were once inexplicable, and god-like powers were attributed to them. Under such conditions, the blotting-out of the sun, the giver of light, the sudden fall of darkness at noon, could only be interpreted as the most evil of omens. Thousands of years passed before it proved possible to explain why such things happened. But even though science has taken the magic (and fortunately, the terror) out of eclipses, they still figure among the most impressive of all natural occurrences. (*Eclipses*)

13. In childhood, showing-off takes simple direct forms. A child asking you to look at him as he stands on his head expects (and usually gets) immediate praise. As we grow older we seem to get more cunning in our

efforts to draw the attention of others to ourselves. Only a professional acrobat has to go to the lengths of standing on his head to win a round of applause. Adults are capable of the subtlest forms of self-dispraise when they want to boast about their achievements. (*On showing-off*)

14. Only in fairly recent times has the idea of climbing a mountain *for its own sake* become general. In the past, mountains were regarded as nothing but ugly, disordered heaps of stone which it would be folly to climb. The successful and dramatic ascent of the Matterhorn in the nineteenth century, did much to change this attitude. Equipped with huge stores of food and barrels of wine to sustain them on their arduous journey, early climbers scaled a great number of peaks in the Alps. Modern mountaineering gear is less bulky but far more complicated. The need for wind-proof clothing, pressure cookers, vacuum packed foods, medical supplies, and nylon ropes has made climbing a formidable undertaking. This often tempts people to ask mountaineers why they go to all this trouble just to climb mountains. Mallory's famous answer, 'Because they're there,' leaves them more puzzled than before. (*Mountaineering*)

15. As soon as we take our place in the queue, our whole outlook on life changes. All we can think about is how many people there are in front of us and how long it will be before our turn comes. Now and then we look back and feel a warm glow of satisfaction when we note how much the queue has lengthened since we joined it. Our main concern, however, is that no one should use unfair means. We keep a watchful eye on the people in front and are ready to denounce publicly anyone who dares to 'jump the queue'. (*On standing in the queue*)

A hundred titles

Instructions

Write essays of between 600 and 800 words on each of the subjects given below. Take special care to *interpret* each topic before you begin planning.

Do not spend more than two hours on each essay. The best way to divide your time is as follows: planning: up to 25 minutes; writing: up to 75 minutes; re-reading and correction: up to 20 minutes.

Choose subjects that really appeal to you. You can do this by immediately eliminating titles which require special knowledge or which you know you cannot attempt. Remember that topics which do not seem particularly attractive at first sight may often provide material for an interesting essay.

1. Fashion.
2. Bridges.

3. On talking to yourself.
4. Eccentrics.
5. On not knowing how to cook.
6. Holidays.
7. House-hunting.
8. Intuition.
9. The ideals of democracy.
10. On giving and receiving presents.
11. On duelling as a way of settling an argument.
12. Relations.
13. Deserts.
14. On meeting your own countrymen abroad.
15. Film stars.
16. A sense of humour.
17. Expectant fathers.
18. On answering children's questions.
19. Watches and clocks.
20. On having to write essays.
21. Cruelty to animals.
22. Telephones.
23. Amateur theatricals.
24. Atomic energy.
25. Patriotism.
26. Intelligence tests.
27. On wearing glasses.
28. Caves.
29. Furnishing a nursery.
30. Country houses.
31. Sportsmanship.
32. New Year's Eve.
33. Bedside lamps.
34. On not being able to draw.
35. Trees.
36. Village gossips.
37. Bargain-hunting.
38. Frontiers.
39. Ash-trays.
40. The sun.
41. On reading detective stories.
42. Knobs.
43. A room of one's own.
44. Cathedrals.
45. Tape-recorders.

46. Books.
47. Food.
48. On being industrious.
49. Other people's worries.
50. Great cities.
51. On being an accomplished person.
52. Prejudice.
53. Corruption.
54. Smoking.
55. Old clothes.
56. Pain.
57. Exiles.
58. Tact.
59. Television.
60. Glass.
61. Gadgets.
62. New car-designs.
63. Self-expression.
64. Maturity.
65. Shadows.
66. The moon.
67. Mime.
68. On cultivating your own garden.
69. Fame.
70. Human nature.
71. Death.
72. Youth clubs.
73. Social insurance.
74. On biting off more than you can chew.
75. Camouflage.
76. Justice.
77. Modesty.
78. On having a man about the house.
79. Hospitality.
80. On having a mind.
81. The gods.
82. Materialism.
83. Luck.
84. On sand and shells.
85. The wisdom of the East.
86. On being curious.
87. Immortality.
88. Peace of mind.

89. The changing landscape.
90. Flower arrangement.
91. Material possessions.
92. Euthanasia.
93. On being lazy.
94. On getting out of the 'rat-race'.
95. The Christmas Tree.
96. On disapproving of the younger generation.
97. Supersonic flight.
98. On being hard of hearing.
99. The week-end.
100. On living to be a hundred.

The argumentative essay

Instructions
An argumentative essay is in many ways similar to an abstract one in that it is concerned almost entirely with *ideas*. But it differs in one important respect: as you are required to discuss a *particular* problem, you are not free to interpret a subject in any way you wish. An ability to reason and a capacity for arranging ideas in logical order are the important requirements of an argumentative essay. In addition to this you must draw largely on your general knowledge: what you *know* is far more important than what you *imagine* or *observe*.

1. AIMS Here are some of the chief things you will be expected to do when writing argumentative essays:
(a) To argue for or against a proposition without necessarily attempting to persuade the reader to agree with you. Your aim here is simply to present a viewpoint.
(b) To argue in such a way as to persuade the reader to agree with you.
(c) To attempt to solve a problem.
(d) To discuss a problem without necessarily arriving at a solution.

2. DEFINING AN ATTITUDE Argumentative topics cannot be interpreted in a wide variety of ways. The *meaning* of a subject is usually immediately clear. There should be no doubt, for instance, about the meaning of the following: 'Is it right that books, plays, and films should be subjected to censorship?' The difficulty here lies not in interpretation, but in deciding on the best way of tackling the subject. It is possible to argue for or against, or to give both viewpoints without committing yourself to one side or the other. Before attempting to make a plan, you must *define your attitude*, that is, you must decide on the way you intend to argue. Sometimes this is not difficult as argumentative topics are often deliberately provocative, taking the form of a challenging quotation like, 'Painting today has become meaningless and childish'. The actual phrasing of the topic often helps you to define a satisfactory attitude.

3. SUBJECT-MATTER The ability to write a good argumentative essay depends not only on what you know but on how well you can use what you know. A few facts which are used well can be far more effective than a great number which do not add anything significant to the essay.

Students who have a wide general knowledge should guard against a tendency to write purely factual prose so that their essays read like articles in an encyclopaedia. Facts should provide nothing more than the framework for ideas, speculations, theories, or opinions. The correct presentation of facts is as important as the facts themselves.

When referring to facts you should take great care to be accurate. Do not 'invent' false facts to prove an idea; do not make vague generalizations. It is equally important to avoid confusion between proved fact and mere opinion.

4. TREATMENT There are two main forms of argument: *inductive* and *deductive*. In 'inductive' argument, you begin with a general statement and then produce facts to prove it. In 'deductive' argument, you infer one statement from another, beginning with a general idea and arriving at a particular one.

Whichever way you choose to argue, you must ensure that your essay is balanced and that you deal with both sides of the argument. This is especially important when you have a definite viewpoint of your own. As a general rule, you should begin by considering the other side of the case first. In this way it is possible to anticipate probable objections to what you have to say. This technique will invariably enable you to present your case in the best way.

Each paragraph should contain a central idea and the sentences should be closely related to each other. Transitions between paragraphs will be smooth if you warn the reader beforehand that you are going to deal with another aspect of the question. Your essay must be a well-organized and balanced whole.

It is easy to understand the function of the *Introduction, Development,* and *Conclusion* if you think of an argumentative essay in terms of a geometrical theorem. You begin with something to prove or to explain; you have a 'given' amount of information (facts); using this information, you go on to your 'proof' either by using facts to prove one or a number of general statements (induction), or by a process of reasoning: inferring one idea from another (deduction). In this way you arrive at a final conclusion which has evolved from the foregoing argument.

(a) *Introduction* This should be devoted to a close examination of the statement. Clear indication of the way you intend to define your attitude should be given to the reader. The whole argument that is to follow will be built on the initial premise which is contained in the introduction.

(b) *Development* Devote the first one or two paragraphs to a consideration of the other side of the case before amplifying your views. From then on, each paragraph you write must add something new and important to your argument.

(c) *Conclusion* Here you may in some way re-state your initial premise.

If you have convincingly 'proved' your case, the premise will have a
new meaning for the reader. If, on the other hand, it has not been
possible to arrive at a satisfactory solution, you should point out why this
is so.

5. DEVICES: *Illustration, Contrast.*

(a) *Illustration* There is always a danger that *purely* deductive argument
will be obscure. An abstract idea will always become clear if a definite
example is given to illustrate it. Supposing, for example, that you are
arguing that more progress has been made in astronomy in the last fifty
years than at any other time in history. You could illustrate this idea by
referring the findings of Copernicus, Galileo, Kepler, and Newton to
explain what was done in the past, and to Einstein, the 200-inch
telescope at Mount Palomar, 'quasars', radio telescopes and radio
satellites to indicate what has been discovered in our own times. Once
you have given an illustration, it is easier to draw a conclusion.

(b) *Contrast* If you are presenting both sides of a case, contrast is
embodied in the very framework of your essay. Try to vary the facts
you use as much as possible. The wider the range of reference, the more
interesting your essay becomes.

6. STYLE Students are often under the impression that difficult
argumentative subjects require an involved style because this will give
their essays the right 'tone'. This leads them to write in a way which is
quite unnatural for them. Keep your English as simple and direct as
possible. A sure way to do this is to write on subjects you are sure you can
handle well. If your ideas are muddled and undigested, this will be reflected in your writing: it will soon be apparent to the reader that you do
not really know what you want to say. Clear thinking and a knowledge of
your subject will enable you to write in a straightforward, readable style.

It is best to avoid the first person except in cases where you are
specifically asked to give your own opinions.

7. PLANNING How you will order your ideas is for you to decide. In any
case, it is essential to make out a full plan before attempting to write your
essay. You may, of course, depart from your original scheme if you have
second thoughts in the course of writing. A sound plan will enable you to
build up an argument in the most effective way and prevent you from
repeating yourself.

When planning, leave a wide margin on the left-hand side of the page.
In the left-hand column, note your ideas in any order as they occur to
you. These notes will provide you with the raw material for your plan
which should be written out on the right. Each paragraph-outline on the
right should consist of a central thought and a few subsidiary ideas
related to it. As you become more and more proficient, it will become less
and less necessary to make out a very detailed plan.

Examine carefully the plan below and note its relation to the essay that follows.

SUBJECT Argue against the view that fine old buildings of no real artistic or historic value should be demolished to make room for modern constructions.

IDEAS	PLAN
Modernization.	*Introduction*
Re-development.	1. The sort of old building that is
Ugly villages.	threatened. Beautiful and ugly.
Real enemies; land	*Development*
speculation.	2. Arguments of those out to demolish
Functional blocks.	old buildings. Unconvincing. Why?
Characterless cities.	3. How the appearance of a city can be
Eighteenth century.	changed for the worse. Lack of
Packing cases.	proportion: mere size.
What is beautiful or	4. Who are the real enemies of old
ugly?	buildings? Speculators: arguments:
National monuments.	modernization etc. and why they seem
Concrete lamps.	convincing.
'Progress'.	5. Charm of big cities: variety. Fine old
	buildings not replaced by equally fine
	modern ones. Functional blocks.
	Monotony.
	Conclusion
	6. Eighteenth century: ruins. Irony
	today.

From time to time, a proposal to pull down a much-loved old building to make room for a factory or a new block of flats, raises a storm of angry protest. Buildings of national importance are relatively safe. Though even these are occasionally threatened, their reputation does protect them to some extent. It is the border-line cases that are always in danger: the dignified buildings of the past which may possess no real artistic or historic value, but which people have become sentimentally attached to and have grown to love. There is no point in calling such buildings 'ugly'. The words 'beautiful' and 'ugly' are relative terms. A building with high ceilings and huge rooms may be less practical than the colourless block of offices that takes its place, but it often fits in well with its surroundings.

Those out to demolish old buildings often argue that a factory will bring prosperity to a town and provide employment for its people; a block of flats will improve living conditions; a new road will create better transport facilities. These arguments are true, but somehow unconvincing. Countless quiet country villages have been spoilt by the addition of modern 'improvements' like huge traffic-signs or tall concrete lamps which shed a sickly yellow light. In the same way, buildings which are erected without any thought being given to their surroundings, become prominent landmarks which may change the character of a whole town. They are ugly because they are so out of place.

Nothing can change the look of a town or city so dramatically as the sudden appearance of a block of offices which towers above all the surrounding buildings. Before the arrival of this skyscraper, all the buildings in the city stood in special relationship to each other. The most imposing of them was probably the cathedral or the town hall followed by other public buildings. These dominated the city and gave it a definite shape. Suddenly, out of nowhere, the new arrival (which is rarely even a public building) dwarfs everything in sight, and even the most graceful and imposing existing buildings may now be so sadly diminished as to seem slightly ridiculous beside this monster. It rises up above them like a huge, white, slotted packing-case resting on its side, demanding attention merely because of its size and not because of any intrinsic worth.

It is seldom realized that very often the biggest enemies of old buildings are not town-planners but ruthless individuals speculating in land. Their sole aim is a quick return of profit and they are not particular about how they will obtain it. They are among the first to point out the necessity for 're-development' and 'modernization' by which they mean replacing old buildings by huge blocks with high rent yields. Unfortunately, people are easily persuaded by fine-sounding arguments for the simple reason that in almost any town, many of the most valuable sites are occupied by the beautiful buildings of the past. Each time the cry is raised, yet another old building is sacrificed in the name of 'progress'.

Part of the charm of a big city lies in the variety of styles that can be seen in the architecture of its buildings. One feels that the city has grown slowly and each age has left its mark. By demolishing buildings of bygone times, we wipe out every vestige of the past forever. In place of infinite variety, we have monotonous uniformity. Rows of houses, each of them different and pleasing with their spacious gardens, are replaced by purely functional blocks of flats which have nothing more to commend them that their over-praised 'modern conveniences'. No one would deny that there are many superb modern buildings which are truly representative of the very best architecture of our age. But these are rarely the utilitarian blocks which are to be found in many cities. The trouble is that every time a fine old building is destroyed, it is not necessarily replaced by an equally fine modern one. If the demolition of buildings is uncontrolled, a fine city is in danger of becoming nothing more than a concrete jungle.

In the eighteenth century there was a time when ruins were deliberately erected to lend charm to the countryside. This is not a practice which even the most fanatical lover of old buildings would defend. But it is curiously ironic that the time has now come when valuable remnants of the past are not only neglected, but threatened with extinction.

Answer these questions:

1. Would you say that the title is deliberately provocative?
2. What is the writer's aim in this essay? (To present a viewpoint? To persuade? To solve a problem? To discuss a problem?)
3. Why was it not necessary for the writer to define an attitude to the topic in this particular instance?
4. Comment on the writer's presentation of facts.
5. Find instances of *inductive* or *deductive* reasoning.
6. Does the introduction give a clear indication of the writer's point of view? What is the writer's premise?
7. Discuss the function of the second paragraph.
8. Does each paragraph add something new to the argument? What?
9. Does the conclusion round off the essay in a satisfactory way? Is the initial premise re-stated?
10. Pick out illustrations which have been used by the writer to make abstract ideas clear. Comment on the effectiveness of the illustrations you choose.
11. Is there any contrast in this essay? Justify your answer.
12. Comment on the writer's range of reference. Is there sufficient variety in this essay?
13. Is the writing simple and clear? Comment on the writer's style.
14. Why is a full plan necessary for an essay of this sort?

The question that follows differs in one important respect from the previous one: you are asked to compare and contrast two different things. The way to do this is *not* to write two short essays on each of the subjects to be compared. There should be comparison and contrast all the way through, *within* each paragraph. Note carefully how this has been done, and how the plan is somewhat different in form from the last one. The same method should be used for all titles of this sort.

SUBJECT 'No matter how good a film is, it can never equal a really
fine play.' Support or attack this view.
ATTITUDE Support this view.

IDEAS	PLAN

IDEAS	CINEMA	THEATRE
Different aims.		
Cinema: techniques:		
scenery, spectacular	*Introduction*	
events; close-ups.	1. Attitudes:	
Cinema replace theatre?	a general comparison	
Saturday afternoon.	*Development*	
Theatre: acting:	2. Presentation	
the main thing.	The past and the	
Presentation.	present (comfort,	
Celluloid.	luxury etc.)	
Dimming lights,	Presentation:	
curtains etc.:	techniques: curtains,	
imitating the theatre.	lights etc.	Hushed expectation.
Actor and audience.	3. Aims:	
	people acting out situations.	
	Resources: time and	More limited: it is
	place; scenery;	the acting that
	variety; spectacular	matters.
	events. Close-ups.	
	Conclusion	
	4. Relationship between actor	
	and audience.	
	Poor film better	
	than bad play.	
	Actors: celluloid.	Immediate contact:
		human feelings.

The arrival of the cinema was once thought to herald the death of the
theatre. As cinemas became more and more widespread, it was argued
that this new, cheap form of entertainment would cause theatres to
close down. Fortunately, this has not happened. The two have
continued to flourish side by side. No matter how often we go to the
cinema, a visit to the theatre is still something special. It requires a
certain amount of preparation. The fact that we have to book seats in
advance and dress a little better than usual, makes going to a play an
occasion. The rarer something is, the more we enjoy it; and this
certainly applies to the theatre. Seeing a play is something quite

different from popping into the local cinema for a couple of hours on a rainy Saturday afternoon.

The cinema has learnt a great deal from the theatre about presentation. Gone are the days when crowds were packed on wooden benches in tumbledown buildings to gape at the antics of silent, jerking figures on a screen, while some poor pianist made frantic efforts to translate the drama into music. These days it is quite easy to find a cinema that surpasses a theatre in luxury. Even in small villages, cinemas are spacious, well-lit and well-ventilated places where one can sit in comfort. The projectionist has been trained to *present* the film in true theatre style. The lights are dimmed slowly to give the audience time to prepare themselves for the film they are to see. Talk drops to a whisper and then fades out altogether. As soon as the cinema is in darkness, spotlights are focused on the curtains which are drawn slowly apart, often to the accompaniment of music, to reveal the title of the film. Everything has been carefully contrived so that the spectator will never actually *see* the naked screen which will remind him all too sharply that what he is about to see is merely shadows flickering on a white board. However much the cinema tries to simulate the conditions in a theatre (and it does it very well), it never fully succeeds. Nothing can equal the awe and sense of hushed expectation which is felt by a theatre audience as the curtain is slowly raised.

Basically, the cinema and the theatre try to do the same thing. They both present people acting out situations which the audience will take to be real. But they differ radically in the *way* they do this. The cinema has huge resources at its disposal. Time and place are no object: we can be carried rapidly from country to country and can be shown a great variety of scenery. What we see is sometimes more important than what we hear. Films often rely for their effect entirely on spectacular happenings which do not require any special acting ability: a raging forest fire, a bridge being blown up while a train is crossing it, or a ship being sunk. The camera can similarly present people from countless different angles. We can be shown an unruly mob, or a single detail like a face, a hand, or even a pair of eyes. The camera can lay special stress on the things it wants us to notice. The theatre, on the other hand, is more limited. It is not possible to present rapid changes of scene. Nor can we concentrate on details: we see the stage as a whole. The setting has a secondary position: it is simply a background for the actors. Acting comes first and the success of a play is measured by the ability of its performers.

A poor film is often far better than a bad play. Pleasant scenery can at least compensate for clumsy acting. But no matter how good a film is, it can never equal a really fine play. The actors on the screen are always celluloid, remote, and a little unreal. In a theatre, however, the actor has immediate contact with his audience: he can move it like a great orator. Each performance he gives is unique and it is this that, in the final count, makes the theatre so superior to the cinema. The lack of scenery becomes unimportant. The actors become identified with the characters they portray. We concentrate on human qualities and forget that they are merely 'acting'. This is something a film can rarely achieve.

Answer these questions:

1. What is the writer's aim in this essay? (To present a viewpoint? To persuade? To solve a problem? To discuss a problem?)
2. Is the title so phrased that it is easy to define an attitude?
3. Comment on the writer's presentation of facts.
4. Find instances of *inductive* or *deductive* reasoning.
5. Which do you think the writer prefers: the cinema or the theatre? Is this preference apparent in the introduction?
6. Examine each paragraph closely and comment on the method the writer uses to convey his preference.
7. Does each paragraph add something new to the argument? What?
8. Is the conclusion appropriate? Why?
9. Pick out examples of (a) illustration; (b) contrast. Comment on their effectiveness.
10. Comment on the writer's range of reference. Is there sufficient variety in this essay?
11. Do you get the impression at the end of the essay that a real *comparison* has been made? Why?
12. Is the writing simple and clear. Comment on the writer's style.
13. How does this essay differ from the previous one?
14. Show the relationship between the plan and the finished essay.

Preliminary exercises

Instructions

Write essays based on the five detailed plans given below. You may depart from the set plans in places if you wish. The length of each essay should be between 600 and 800 words. You should spend about an hour and a half on each essay (up to 70 minutes writing; up to 20 minutes re-reading and correcting).

1. SUBJECT   'The application of science to entertainment has made us lazy.' Discuss.

   ATTITUDE   True up to a point; but today there are new forms of self-entertainment; creative energy is used elsewhere.

IDEAS	PLAN
Records.	*Introduction*
TV.	1. Today, more leisure than ever before:
Films.	mass entertainment has become an
Theatre.	'industry'. We are dependent on others
Photography and	for our entertainment, but science has
painting.	also provided new outlets for creative
Books: digests.	energy.
New scope:	*Development*
tape-recorders.	2. The nineteenth century: drawing-room
Entertainment: an	entertainment. Victorian ideal: the
industry.	'accomplished person' and what that
'Accomplishments'.	meant. Very rare today.
Application of	3. How science has been applied:
science: how?	Music making: gramophone versus piano.
Creative energy used	Theatre etc.: films and TV versus
elsewhere: 'do it	amateur theatricals.
yourself'.	Visual arts: photography versus
Victorian times.	painting.
Amateurs.	Reading: newspapers, magazines, and

digests versus books.

4. Effect of this on people: though many
do still paint and play the piano etc., it
would be true to say that we are
dependent on professional entertainers
more than ever before: TV in the home;
the cinema. In this respect we are lazier
than our Victorian counterparts.

5. *But* science has provided new forms of
self-entertainment. Tremendous scope
for the individual in photography,
tape-recording, amateur film-making;
cars: access to the countryside.

Conclusion

6. We have become accustomed to
entertainment of a very high standard
and cannot compete. We are lazy in that
we expect others to entertain us, but
creative energy is used elsewhere: e.g.:
'do it yourself'. Side by side with the
professional, there is great scope for the
amateur.

2. SUBJECT 'To be prepared for war is the most effectual means of preserving peace.' Discuss.

ATTITUDE Argue against this statement.

IDEAS	PLAN
First World War.	*Introduction*
Second World War.	1. Consideration of curious paradox that peace can be maintained by preparing for war. This method for preserving peace has been used throughout the history of man. Rare instances: long periods of peace; but method has never really succeeded.
'Arms race'.	
'Massive retaliation'.	
Meaning of war today.	
Paradox.	
Direction we are moving in.	*Development*
War by accident.	2. Why this outlook prevails: based on belief that other nations are fundamentally aggressive. Mutual suspicion. Balance of power maintained by armaments.
Stock-piling.	
Deliberate aggression.	
Suspicion.	
Roman Empire.	3. Instances when the method has been successful: Roman Empire: 'pax Romana'. Very long period of peace, but the price was domination by a foreign power. Ultimate collapse. Similarly 'pax Britannica' in nineteenth century.
Why outlook prevails.	
'pax Britannica'.	
	4. But the opposite is usually true: e.g. World Wars I and II: general preparedness led directly to war.
	5. The position today. Difference between 'conventional' and 'nuclear' arms. New meaning of war: complete annihilation. But attitude still prevails: 'arms race', 'massive retaliation'. Missiles and counter-missiles. 'Escalation'.
	6. Greatly increased chances of war by accident. (This was less likely in the past.)
	Conclusion
	7. World leaders making a determined effort to disarm. Perhaps we are beginning to understand that the surest road to war is to be prepared for it.

3. SUBJECT 'We should give up trying to reach other planets and
devote ourselves to improving conditions on earth.'
Discuss.
   ATTITUDE Argue against.

IDEAS	PLAN
Vast sums.	*Introduction*
Social services.	1. A tempting argument but
Planets/Moon.	fundamentally mistaken. Why? Imposes
Useful results.	limits; opposes scientific and
Satellites.	technological research.
Opposing progress.	*Development*
Convincing argument.	2. Main reason for opposition: colossal
Imposing limits.	sums spent on space research. Results
'Useless' knowledge.	have a prestige value only. Countries
World population.	engaged do not share knowledge and
Prestige values.	this leads to further waste.
	3. Critics of space research argue that
	money should be employed elsewhere:
	raising living-standards in underdeveloped
	countries; providing social services. Man's
	biggest enemy is poverty, not non-existent
	inhabitants of other worlds.
	4. Convincing but unimaginative
	arguments. The thrill of recent advances.
	Examples: moon, Venus, satellites, men
	in orbit, etc. Rapid progress because
	prestige values provide incentive.
	5. Despite good intentions, arguments
	against space research are mistaken. At
	any period in the past it would have
	been possible to argue that money spent
	on scientific research could have been
	used elsewhere. If this attitude had
	prevailed, there would never have been
	any progress.
	6. It is quite possible that space probes
	will have practical results. Not absurd
	to say that mass-emigration might be a
	solution for over-populated earth. Other
	possible useful results we cannot foresee.

Conclusion
7. Space research is right and natural.
It has grown out of all the scientific
research of the past. There can never be
any justification for imposing restrictions
on man's desire for knowledge. No such
thing as 'useless' knowledge.

4. SUBJECT 'No man is an island entire of itself.' (John Donne)
Discuss.
ATTITUDE Argue in favour.

IDEAS	PLAN
Essential loneliness. Striving to communicate. Effect of others on human personality. Work and play. Art: painting, music and writing: what they represent. Human relationships. Marriage etc. Stimulation of human contact. Teams. Citizen's Advice Bureau.	*Introduction* 1. People are 'islands' in the sense that no two human beings can be completely alike. But even the most primitive individual must feel himself to be part of a community. The idea of *belonging* is deeply ingrained in man: race, nation, city, town, village, family. *Development* 2. Distinguish between loneliness and 'man as an island'. Many lonely people (Citizen's Advice Bureau, a necessity), but no man is an island, not even a hermit. No one can exist as a human being if he has been denied all human contact. 3. Contact means influence. A person's personality considered as the sum total of all the people he has known plus something of his own. Effect of home environment; school; 'the world'. 4. Basic unit is the family. Marriage as an institution. The idea of a 'team' in its widest sense. 5. Meeting other people in work and play satisfies an inmost need: human contact is stimulating and helps us to maintain a sense of proportion. 6. People nearest to being 'islands' are

the most creative: arts and sciences. But
even these spend most of their lives trying
to communicate their ideas to others and
are never free from the influence of
others.
Conclusion
7. Moral codes, laws, administration of
countries based on assumption that we
have much in common as human beings:
'All cases are unique, and very similar
to others.' (T. S. Eliot)

5. SUBJECT 'A scientist can hardly be given credit because he happened
to make a chance discovery.' Discuss.
ATTITUDE Argue against.

IDEAS	PLAN
Fleming.	*Introduction*
Newton.	1. A critical examination of the
Röntgen.	statement. Absurdity of this attitude.
Safety glass.	What is the use of chance without the
Scientific method.	presence of a trained observer? Many
The trained and	examples.
untrained mind.	*Development*
Deliberately setting out	2. According to this statement, credit
to discover something;	can only be given to those who
finding something else.	deliberately set out to discover something
Work of a lifetime.	and succeed.
	3. This view is erroneous because failure
	is as much a part of an experiment as
	success. Successful experiments often
	follow countless unsuccessful ones. Or
	important discoveries are sometimes made
	when a scientist is looking for something
	else. Examples: Röntgen and X-rays;
	Fleming and penicillin.
	4. Why should the scientist be given
	credit for pure chance? Making use of a
	lifetime's training and experience. The
	Scientific Method. The reason why results
	are obtained.
	5. Proof of above by example. Newton.

being struck by an apple; this would
have been meaningless to anyone else.
Accidental discovery of shatter-proof glass
by Benedictus in 1904.
Conclusion
6. Many discoveries may be made by
accident. But it is no accident that a
trained scientist is able to draw
significant conclusions from chance
occurrences.

Exercises

Instructions
Write essays using each of the paragraphs given below. Each paragraph
supplies you with a certain amount of information about the subject.
Using this as a starting-point, you should construct a full and detailed
plan of your own. These paragraphs are not necessarily 'first' or 'last'.
You will be able to see how they fit into the general scheme only after
you have made your plan. The subject of each essay is given in brackets.

You should spend up to two hours on each essay and the length
should be between 600 and 800 words (not including the number of
words in the set paragraphs). You are advised to divide your time as
follows: planning: up to 25 minutes; writing: up to 75 minutes;
re-reading and correction: up to 20 minutes.

1. In this way, mass-production has brought with it a sharp division
between work and pleasure. The modern worker cannot, like the
craftsman before him, enjoy what he is doing. On the other hand,
shorter working-hours coupled with secure employment, leave him an
amount of free time that his predecessors never enjoyed. And modern
industry has so revolutionized methods of transport and entertainment,
that it provides the worker with numerous activities he can devote his
leisure time to. If he uses his spare time wisely and not just as a means
for 'letting off steam' after a dull day's work, he can be more than
compensated for this dissociation of work and pleasure. ('*Mass-
production has had a profound effect on everyday life.*' *Discuss.*)

2. Apart from their intrinsic interest, these studies do show that,
regardless of race, colour, or creed, human beings, even the most
primitive, face more or less the same problems but have different ways
of dealing with them. (*Can anthropological studies carried out among primitive
tribes throw any light on our own way of life?*)

3. Far from encouraging a student to read widely, an examination
syllabus often has the opposite effect. By interpreting a subject in a

special way so that it will conform to some preconceived pattern, it often imposes deliberate restrictions on a student's reading. When the time comes for the student to be examined, he is not necessarily tested on his knowledge of a subject, but on how well he has mastered a few texts. And this is not the only way the examination system defeats its own purposes. Another drawback is that a student is not tested on what he really knows, but is asked to display his knowledge in a special way and in a limited time. In other words, if he wishes to succeed, he has to develop a special technique for answering questions. (*Discuss the system of written examinations as a fair means of testing knowledge.*)

4. Nothing worth having is free in the sense that it can be had without effort. If we wish to acquire one thing, something else must be given in exchange for it. What we give cannot always be measured in terms of money. It can take many forms like time, effort, hard work, or concentration, for only by giving is it possible to receive. In fact, it is doubtful whether anything which appears to be 'free' is really worth having. ('*The best things in life are free.*' *Are they?*)

5. Though people are much less superstitious nowadays than they used to be, they do sometimes give way to illogical fears. The desire to believe in the supernatural lurks in the background and occasionally breaks to the surface. Because superstition is infectious, popular imagination, once fired, needs little encouragement to turn fancy into fact. Some time ago, people claimed to have seen saucer-shaped objects which were supposed to have come from outer space. One writer went so far as to claim that one of these objects landed in a field and that he was able to communicate with diminutive 'people' from Venus. In time, so many of these 'saucers' were seen, that one was led to believe that the earth was threatened with imminent invasion. ('*People are as superstitious today as they ever were in the past.*' *Discuss.*)

6. One solution to this problem is to discourage children from leaving school early. Parents are often to blame for this. Having no conception of what a school can do for a child beyond teaching him how to read, write, and count, they often actually persuade their children to take jobs. Sometimes they are unwilling or unable to make the sacrifices necessary to keep a child at school a year or two longer. Plenty of work is available for boys and girls of sixteen. And free time plus a good supply of pocket-money are great temptations which lure them away from school. Here, again, parents are unable to give proper advice and the children have their own way. ('*Popular education has created a vast, half-educated majority that knows* how *to read, but does not know* what *to read.*' *Discuss.*)

7. Let loose in a supermarket, the bewildered housewife must find it impossible to choose wisely. If she sets out to buy a packet of soap-

powder she is faced with an astonishing range of makes and brand-names. One announces that a free gift-voucher goes with each packet; another that there is a free gift inside; another that the buyer is offered a twenty-per-cent discount if she buys three packets at once; another declares that a new 'easy-to-pour' gadget is attached to the packet. Words, too, do not always mean what they say. Who would guess that 'giant size' often means the smallest package available, or that 'super-economy size' the largest? The way things are at present, it is becoming increasingly impossible for the housewife to assess whether she is getting true value for money. (*'Value for money.' Is there any such thing?*)

8. Part of the difficulty is that the countries which need to take in immigrants are interested in getting as many well-educated, highly-skilled people as possible. On the other hand, the countries capable of providing the greatest number of people are often poor and under-developed so that most of the hopeful emigrants have nothing more to offer than their unskilled labour. The result of this is that the more developed countries rarely use up their 'quota' of potential emigrants, while the less developed ones not only exceed it, but have an enormous waiting-list. (*Discuss the advantages and disadvantages of emigration.*)

9. Today young people seem to be anxious to acquire useful knowledge to the exclusion of everything else. They seek knowledge not for its own sake, but so that they will learn how to do a job. But knowledge and education are not one and the same thing. A man may be in command of any number of facts and be brilliant at his job without necessarily being an educated person. Those who measure knowledge solely in terms of its usefulness often deliberately ignore the immense cultural heritage of the past when they regard the study of Latin and Greek as a 'waste of time'. (*Is it to be regretted that the study of classical languages is becoming less common in our times?*)

10. It took nothing less than two world wars for women to prove conclusively that they are capable of doing any kind of job, from serving as Minister of Health to driving a steam-roller. Yet men are still reluctant to acknowledge that women are as capable as they are, and not a few must wish that they had never been given the vote at all. It is fortunate for women, these days, that they do not have to chain themselves to lamp-posts or starve themselves to death to prove a simple point. If they go about it the right way, they might even beat men to the moon. (*' There are still certain professions from which women should be excluded.' Discuss.*)

11. Statistics have to be correctly interpreted if they are to be of value. They are often the result of prolonged and painstaking scientific

research and can provide really valuable information about population density, conditions in industry, the weather, road accidents, and countless other aspects of everyday life. Quite frequently, statisticians go to great lengths to verify what seems to be obvious to everyone. Nothing is true unless it is proved to be so. This is precisely what makes statistics so valuable: everyone might be aware that a problem exists, but only accurate figures can indicate its extent and suggest what might be the best way of coping with it. (*'You can prove anything with statistics.' Is this a fair comment?*)

12. This is precisely why the sham Gothic architecture of the nineteenth century seems so absurd to us today. It does not represent its age and is only a poor imitation of the past. Nothing could be more ridiculous than the grubby railway station which pretends to be a Gothic cathedral. Even a drab Victorian factory is preferable to this. At least it does not pretend to be something else. It honestly reflects its time and the conditions under which it was built. The only thing the 'baroque' hotel or 'High Renaissance' public building can reflect is the lack of originality and the poor taste of their designers. (*To what extent should the architecture of any period reflect its age?*)

13. The critic, then, has a twofold function: he must illuminate and evaluate. The first of these is quite straightforward. Acting as an intermediary between the artist and the public, a critic should be able to explain the intentions behind a book, a film, a play, or whatever it is he is criticizing. If the critic is reliable we should be better equipped to enjoy say, a new novel, after we have read what he has to say. The second is far more difficult. When attempting to evaluate a work of art, the critic should be able to see it in relation to all that has gone before and to give his readers some indication of its possible worth. What he gives us, in effect, is his opinion; and more often than not, there are as many opinions as there are critics. (*Attempt to define the business of the critic.*)

14. No one would underestimate the importance of inventions like these, but the really great invention is the one which has made others possible. Man's greatest inventions have not grown out of laboratories or workshops. Their origins are obscure. No one can be sure exactly when the needle, or the plough, came into existence, but one thing is certain: we depend on inventions like these today as much as we did at any time in the past. They have become an indispensable part of life on earth, and some like the wheel, the alphabet and Arabic numerals underlie all the progress of recent years. (*What, in your view, is the greatest invention of all time?*)

15. For this sort of traveller, the present does not exist. The happiest moments of arrival which should be landmarks in his life he never

notices because he always hopes for something better. What, exactly, it is he is hoping for, it is doubtful whether he himself knows. He never experiences uninhibited pleasure, for happiness is always just beyond his reach. Without his noticing, the whole of life goes by, and at the end of it all, he is left only with hopes which will never be fulfilled. (' *To travel hopefully is better than to arrive.*' *R. L. Stevenson. Discuss.*)

A hundred subjects

Instructions
Write essays of between 600 and 800 words on each of the subjects given below. Take special care to *define an attitude* to each topic before you begin planning.

Do not spend more than two hours on each essay. The best way to divide your time is as follows: planning: up to 25 minutes; writing: up to 75 minutes; re-reading and correction: up to 20 minutes.

Choose subjects that really appeal to you. You can do this by immediately eliminating titles which require special knowledge or which you know you cannot attempt. Remember that topics which do not seem particularly attractive at first sight may often provide material for an interesting essay.

1. Would it be true to say that national character is largely influenced by climate?
2. Do you think that a politically and economically united Europe is desirable?
3. 'Religion is the opium of the people.' (Marx) Discuss.
4. 'There can be no freedom without discipline.' Discuss.
5. Discuss the effect of the Press on public opinion.
6. 'All art is useless.' (Oscar Wilde) Discuss.
7. 'Every man is the architect of his own future.' Argue in favour of this statement.
8. 'It is unfortunate that English, which has for some time been the most widely used language in the world – the chief language of trade, and the national or administrative language of six hundred million people – should be so difficult a one – and that there should be no short cuts to learning it.' (Robert Graves and Alan Hodge) Discuss.
9. Discuss the uses and abuses of strikes.
10. Is capital punishment defensible?
11. 'Read not to contradict and confute, nor to believe and take for granted, nor to find talk and discourse, but to weigh and consider.' (Francis Bacon) Discuss the purpose of reading.
12. 'All history is current history.' Argue for or against this statement.

13. The twentieth century has often been called 'the age of the common man'. What is your view?

14. Is the influence of comic papers on young minds wholly undesirable?

15. 'The best lack all conviction, while the worst
    Are full of passionate intensity.' (W. B. Yeats)
    Discuss.

16. Account for the rapid growth of world population in the last hundred years and discuss some of the main problems this will give rise to.

17. 'Propaganda is the worst form of argument.' Would you agree?

18. 'Good writing cannot be popular today; and popular writing cannot genuinely explore experience.' (Richard Hoggart) Discuss.

19. Would it be true to say that the idea of family life has changed radically in the last fifty or so years?

20. '... when a scientist gets loose into the field of religion, all that he can do is to give us the impression which his scientific knowledge and thought has produced upon his everyday, and usually commonplace, personal and private imagination.' (T. S. Eliot) Discuss.

21. 'Equality of opportunity.' Can there ever really be such a thing?

22. 'Everything that enlarges the sphere of human powers, that shows man he can do what he thought he could not do, is valuable.' (Dr Samuel Johnson) Discuss.

23. 'Country life is less impersonal than town life.' Would you agree with this statement?

24. What are the chief natural resources of your country and would you say they are effectively exploited?

25. Is a hereditary monarchy an anachronism today?

26. Can pain and suffering be of any value?

27. 'Good fences make good neighbours.' (Robert Frost) Consider the implications of this statement.

28. What would you consider to be the greatest contribution your country has made to the civilized world?

29. 'We do not say that a man who takes no interest in politics minds his own business. We say he has no business here at all.' (Pericles) Discuss.

30. Prevention is better than cure.' Consider this statement in the light of recent advances in the field of medicine.

31. 'The end justifies the means.' Discuss.

32. What do you understand by the terms Classical and Romantic?

33. Suggest reasons for the sharp rise in juvenile delinquency since the war.

34. 'The mind is in its own place, and in itself
    Can make a Heaven of Hell, a Hell of Heaven.' (Milton)
    Discuss.
35. 'The human race's prospects of survival were considerably better
    when we were defenceless against tigers than they are today when
    we have become defenceless against ourselves.' (Arnold Toynbee)
    Discuss.
36. Is it right that the main industries and services of a country should
    be controlled by the State?
37. Should books, plays and films be subjected to censorship?
38. 'Money, with no strings attached.' Is this the best contribution
    the wealthier nations can make to their poorer neighbours?
39. 'Advertising is one of the most unpleasant features of modern life.'
    Argue for or against this statement.
40. Place the arts in order.
41. 'Psychical research has produced nothing but a mass of conflicting
    evidence.' Discuss.
42. 'You get what you pay for.' Is this a fair comment on the taxation
    system that operates in your country?
43. Discuss the differences between Classical music and Jazz, indicating
    which you prefer and why.
44. 'Diplomacy is mainly the interplay of the domestic problems of
    many countries.' (Sir David Ormsby Gore) Discuss.
45. How necessary is peace-time conscription?
46. Would you say that the measures taken to prevent road accidents
    in your country are adequate?
47. 'The essence of wisdom is emancipation, as far as possible, from the
    tyranny of the here and the now.' (Bertrand Russell) Discuss.
48. What is to be said in support of the view that criminals should be
    treated as if they were mentally ill?
49. 'A little learning is a dangerous thing.' Would you agree?
50. 'Work is more fun than fun.' (Noël Coward) Discuss.
51. 'The arts can only truly flourish in prosperous communities.' Is
    there any truth in this statement?
52. Is a dictatorship ever justifiable?
53. 'Seeing is believing.' Is this an adequate philosophical attitude?
54. 'When prosperity knocks at the door, communication flies out of
    the window.' Consider this statement with reference to personal
    relationships and explain what you understand by it.
55. Would it be true to say that young people specialize too early today
    and therefore fail to acquire a broad education?
56. It is often said that we have progressed a great deal today. What,
    in your view, is the essence of progress?

5

57. 'Nobody ought to own houses or furniture – any more than they own the stones of the high road.' (D. H. Lawrence) Discuss.

58. Discuss the importance of tourism as a source of income to your country.

59. 'You cannot bully Nature.' Argue in favour of this statement.

60. What, in your opinion, should be the qualities of an ideal civil servant?

61. Write a critical account of any three daily newspapers published in your country.

62. 'Democracy is a word which grumbles meaninglessly in empty bellies.' (Ritchie Calder) Discuss.

63. 'A crime may be a sin, but a sin is not necessarily a crime.' Discuss.

64. Argue against the view that it is impossible for the underdeveloped nations ever to catch up with their more advanced neighbours.

65. 'Automation is likely to create more problems than ever before.' Discuss.

66. 'Teaching machines have come to stay.' Is this desirable?

67. Are there ever occasions when it is right for the State to interfere with the private life of an individual?

68. 'A man must carry knowledge with him, if he would bring home knowledge.' (Dr Samuel Johnson). Consider this statement with special reference to the modern tourist.

69. Consider the effectiveness of the United Nations Organization as an instrument for maintaining peace.

70. 'Fascism and Communism are more closely related than they would appear to be.' Discuss.

71. Is the idea of the 'noble savage' simply a myth?

72. Is a truly successful marriage an unattainable ideal?

73. Would you say that it is wrong to encourage the sort of 'betting' that is promoted by national lotteries and football pools?

74. Assess the importance of home environment in the formation of character.

75. Is a country justified in maintaining a secret intelligence service?

76. 'People are always good company when they are doing what they really enjoy.' (Samuel Butler) Discuss.

77. To what extent have modern means of communication altered the pattern of our daily lives during this century?

78. Can you foresee any possible changes in the present balance of power within the next fifty years?

79. 'What should concern us is not the city of today, but the city of the future.' Discuss.

80. What can be said in support of the view that in our efforts to control pests we are seriously altering the balance of nature?

81. 'The human mind has been equipped with a wonderful capacity for accepting evidence which agrees with its preconceptions.' (Peter Opie) Discuss.
82. 'Familiarity breeds contempt.' Discuss.
83. 'The balanced individual ... must know his origins, understand his background; appreciate the people, the historic processes, and the circumstances of which he is the contemporary projection.' (Morris Adler) Discuss.
84.   'What is this life if, full of care,
    We have no time to stand and stare.' (W. H. Davies)
Discuss.
85. 'Broadcasting should never be a monopoly.' Discuss.
86. 'The car is going to contribute very largely to wrecking our civilization.' (Alec Issigonis) Discuss.
87. '... conscience does make cowards of us all.' (Shakespeare) Discuss.
88. 'Modern painting gives plenty of scope to the charlatan.' Discuss.
89. Would it be true to say that most fairy tales are unsuitable reading-matter for young children?
90. 'The history of heroes is the history of youth.' (Disraeli) Discuss.
91. How far does language reflect national character? Consider this with reference to your own language and to English.
92. Is there any point in trying to build cities under the sea? Discuss this with reference to recent developments in undersea exploration.
93. Are film stars worth the enormous sums they are paid?
94. 'The future is ... black.' (James Baldwin)
'We will learn to live together like brothers or we will perish together like fools.' (Martin Luther King)
Consider one or both these statements with reference to racial discrimination.
95. 'Boxing cannot, in any sense of the word, be called a sport.' Discuss.
96. Imagine that you are living in 2080 A.D. Write an essay entitled 'The Twentieth Century'.
97. Consider the claim of photography to be judged at the same level as painting or drawing.
98. 'One man's gnat is another man's camel.' (Samuel Butler) Discuss.
99. Poetic language is 'current language heightened, to any degree heightened and unlike itself, but not an obsolete one.' (G. M. Hopkins)
'The language of the age is never the language of poetry.' (Thomas Gray)
Which view would you support and why?
100. Do we ever really learn from our mistakes?

The literary essay (advanced)

Poetry

Instructions

1. READING If you are studying the works of a major poet, you will find it impossible to become fully acquainted with *all* the poems included in the selection. You should, therefore, concentrate on the most important ones and make it your aim to know them well. You will be required to have a detailed knowledge of these poems and they will have to be read several times before they can be properly assimilated. Minor poems should not be ignored, but less emphasis should be placed on them.

2. SUMMARIES It is essential to keep a record of each of the major poems you read. The notes you make on each poem should fall into three distinct parts:

(a) *Meaning and Intention* A brief, stanza by stanza summary should be made, together with a short note on the poet's intention.

(b) *Structure* Note should be made of any outstanding structural features, principally the following: Contrast, Illustration, and Repetition.

(c) *Devices* Any of the following will be found in the poems you read: Simile, Metaphor, Personification, Alliteration, Onomatopoeia, Rhyme, Assonance, and Rhythm. Keep a record of a few useful quotations which illustrate any of these devices.

Study Keats' Ode 'To Autumn' which is given below. When you have done so, read carefully the notes which follow, noting how they have been written.

To Autumn

I

Season of mists and mellow fruitfulness,
  Close bosom-friend of the maturing sun;
Conspiring with him how to load and bless
  With fruit the vines that round the thatch-eves run;
To bend with apples the moss'd cottage-trees,
  And fill all fruit with ripeness to the core;
    To swell the gourd, and plump the hazel shells
  With a sweet kernel; to set budding more,
And still more, later flowers for the bees,
Until they think warm days will never cease,
    For Summer has o'er-brimm'd their clammy cells.

II

Who hath not seen thee oft amid thy store?
  Sometimes whoever seeks abroad may find
Thee sitting careless on a granary floor,
  Thy hair soft-lifted by the winnowing wind;
Or on a half-reap'd furrow sound asleep,
  Drows'd with the fume of poppies, while thy hook
    Spares the next swath and all its twined flowers:
And sometimes like a gleaner thou dost keep
  Steady thy laden head across a brook;
  Or by a cyder-press, with patient look,
    Thou watchest the last oozings hours by hours.

III

Where are the songs of Spring? Ay, where are they?
  Think not of them, thou hast thy music too, –
While barred clouds bloom the soft-dying day,
  And touch the stubble-plains with rosy hue;
Then in a wailful choir the small gnats mourn
  Among the river sallows, borne aloft
    Or sinking as the light wind lives or dies;
And full-grown lambs loud bleat from hilly bourn;
  Hedge-crickets sing; and now with treble soft
  The red-breast whistles from a garden-croft;
    And gathering swallows twitter in the skies.

NOTES

(a) *Meaning and Intention*

Stanza I Picture of the richness of autumn: vines, apples, gourd, hazel shells, late flowers: the end of summer.

Stanza II Where autumn may be 'seen': the 'granary floor', the 'half-reap'd furrow', the brook, the 'cyder-press'.

Stanza III The songs of spring – but there is also 'music' in autumn: at the end of the day: sound of gnats, lambs, crickets, the red-breast, swallows.

Intention To re-create the atmosphere of autumn and to convey its richness and beauty.

(b) *Structure* The poem is built on illustrations which convey the main idea behind each stanza (e.g. apple trees, the 'cyder-press', the 'full-grown lambs'). Brief contrast with spring in Stanza III.

(c)   *Devices*

Simile	'... like a gleaner thou dost keep
	Steady thy laden head across a brook'.
Metaphor	'... Summer has o'er-brimm'd their clammy cells'.
	'Drowsed with the fume of poppies'.
	'... in a wailful choir the small gnats mourn'.
Personification	'... whoever seeks abroad may find
	Thee sitting careless on a granary floor,' etc.
Alliteration	'winnowing wind'.
	'... barred clouds bloom the soft-dying day'.
	'... lambs loud bleat from hilly bourn'.
Rhyme	Strict pattern, but not insistent.
Rhythm	Drowsy: closely matches sense.

3. FURTHER STUDY When you have completed your notes on each poem, you should attempt to see the poet's work *as a whole*. The chief things you should observe are as follows:

(a) The main themes that recur in the poet's work and which poems best illustrate them.

(b) The principal features of the poet's style (e.g. use of metaphor; everyday speech; satire; attention to detail etc.). It should not be necessary for you at this stage to refer to works of criticism. Pay close attention to the actual poems rather than to what other people have to say about them.

4. PLANNING Your plan must be a close and accurate analysis of the question. In the column on the left, write down the titles of the poems and the ideas which you consider relevant to the question. On the right, divide your essay into main headings, noting the poems you will use to illustrate your ideas. Your general attitude to the subject should be defined in the introduction.

The plan and essay given below are based on a selection of Keats' poetry. Study them carefully, noting how they have been written.

SUBJECT   Would it be true to say that in his Odes, Keats attempts to escape from the unhappiness of life through some form of delight in beautiful sights and sounds?

ATTITUDE   Statement true only for 'Nightingale' and 'Grecian Urn'.

TITLES AND IDEAS	PLAN
'Psyche'.	*Introduction*
'Autumn'.	1. Statement true only for 'Nightingale'
'Urn'.	and 'Grecian Urn'.
'Melancholy'.	*Development*
'Nightingale'.	2. Beautiful sights and sounds but no
Identification.	symbolism: 'Psyche' and 'Autumn'.
Beautiful sights	3. Unhappiness felt keenly:
and sounds.	'Melancholy'; escape implied?
Symbolism and lack	4. Escape theme in 'Nightingale' and
of symbolism.	'Urn'.
Escape theme.	5. 'Nightingale': identification with
Escape from what?	beautiful object: *sound*.
	6. 'Urn': identification with beautiful
	object: *sights*.
	Conclusion
	7. Harsh reality: escape temporary.

Though Keats' great love for the beauty of Nature and classical
mythology can be seen in all his Odes, it is only in the Odes 'To a
Nightingale' and 'On a Grecian Urn' that he gives direct expression
to his desire to escape from the unhappiness of life on earth.

Keats conveys this love of beautiful sights and sounds in the 'Ode to
Psyche' and 'To Autumn'. In 'Psyche', the lovers are discovered
> 'In deepest grass, beneath the whisp'ring roof
> Of leaves and trembled blossoms'.

The poem 'To Autumn' is full of beautiful pictures and sounds: 'the
small gnats mourn', the 'lambs loud bleat from hilly bourn'. But in
both poems, Keats is interested in beautiful objects for their own sakes.
The beauties described do not at the same time symbolize a more
perfect world to which the poet may escape.

In the 'Ode to Melancholy', Keats urges the reader to contemplate
intensely beautiful and ephemeral objects in order to feel unhappiness
more keenly, not to escape from it. At the same time, there is an implied
suggestion of 'escape' into a more beautiful world. One is not wholly
unhappy when considering 'beauty that must die', but experiences
'aching Pleasure'.

Direct expression of the desire for escape from the world is given in the
Odes 'To a Nightingale' and 'On a Grecian Urn'. In the former
poem, Keats speaks of the misery on earth:
> 'The weariness, the fever, and the fret
> Here, where men sit and hear each other groan'.

Similarly, human love in 'On a Grecian Urn' is undesirable because it

> '... leaves a heart high-sorrowful and cloy'd,
> A burning forehead, and a parching tongue.'

In both these Odes, Keats identifies himself with some 'unworldly' beautiful object. Real beauty, according to the poet, is immortal and, therefore, beyond the range of human experience. For an instant, the beautiful song of the nightingale enables him to become one with objects of great beauty: '... the Queen Moon ... Cluster'd around by all her starry Fays'. The description of Nature that follows in the stanza beginning 'I cannot see what flowers are at my feet,' is both realistic and symbolic of Keats' conception of absolute beauty, and differs in this respect from similar descriptions in 'To Autumn'.

If beautiful sounds help the poet to escape from 'leaden-eyed despairs' in the 'Ode to a Nightingale', beautiful sights enable him to do the same in the Ode 'On a Grecian Urn'. Here Keats reconstructs an ancient scene which, for him, has absolute beauty because it is eternal:

> 'Ah, happy, happy boughs! that cannot shed
> Your leaves, nor ever bid the Spring adieu'.

For a short time, Keats is able to identify himself so completely with the 'little town' he imagines that he forgets the unhappiness of the world.

The harsh reality of everyday life, however, is always in the background. In the 'Ode to a Nightingale', 'the plaintive anthem fades' to 'toll' the poet back to his 'sole self'. 'On a Grecian Urn' likewise ends with a reference to old age and passing generations:

> 'When old age shall this generation waste,
> Thou shalt remain, in midst of other woe
> Than ours ...'

Escape from this world can never be anything more than momentary.

Answer these questions:

1. Explain, with reference to the above essay, how a study of the meaning, intention, structure, and devices of each poem help the writer to answer the question.
2. Comment on the arrangement of material in this essay and on the writer's use of fact.
3. What is the function of the Introduction and how do the paragraphs that follow develop the main idea?
4. Would it be true to say that this is an *exact* answer to the question set? Why?
5. Show what relationship exists between the plan and the finished essay.

Exercises

Instructions

Where relevant, the questions below should be answered with reference to any selection of poems you have studied in detail. You should write essays of between 350 and 500 words and not spend more than 45 minutes on each question. The best way to divide your time is as follows: planning: 5–10 minutes; writing: 30–35 minutes; re-reading: 5–10 minutes.

1. Give an account of the poet's power as a story-teller.
2. Discuss the poet's sympathy with Nature.
3. Illustrate the poet's concern for human thoughts and feelings.
4. Discuss the poet's interest in the past.
5. Give an account of the poet's ability as a descriptive writer, pointing out his attention to detail.
6. What has the poet to say about his own personal feelings and experiences?
7. Write a detailed appreciation of any *two* lyrics.
8. Write a detailed appreciation of any *two* poems which contrast with each other in style and subject-matter.
9. What is the poet's attitude to good and evil?
10. Illustrate any three of the following from your knowledge of the poems: (i) vivid description; (ii) vigorous action; (iii) sorrow and despair; (iv) family affection; (v) peaceful scenes.
11. Account for the poet's optimism or pessimism.
12. What evidence is there of inner conflict in the poems you have studied?
13. What would you consider to be the poet's favourite subject?
14. Discuss the poet's use of metaphor.
15. What special interests has the poet? (e.g. love of music, mythology, nature etc.). Illustrate your answer from your knowledge of the poems.
16. Basing your answer on *four* or *five* poems, give an account of the poet's view of life.
17. Do we learn anything about contemporary events from this selection of poems?
18. Write a full appreciation of any *one* longer poem you have studied.
19. What is more important to the poet: sensations or thoughts?
20. Discuss the poet's attitude to human relationships.
21. What religious feeling is expressed in the poems you have read?
22. Discuss the main features of the poet's style.
23. Is a consistent philosophy of life expressed in the poems you have read?

24. What appeals most to the poet: a life of action, or one of meditation?
25. Discuss the poet's attitude to death and after-life.
26. Describe the function of different backgrounds and settings in any *five* poems you have read.
27. What is the poet's attitude to everyday things?
28. Discuss and illustrate the poet's qualities as a satirist.
29. 'A reading of the minor poetry is indispensable to a proper understanding of the major poetry.' Discuss.
30. What is more important to the poet: the detailed description of scenes, or the thoughts that these scenes suggest to him?

Plays and novels

1. SUMMARIES It is essential to make brief notes of the contents of any play or novel you are studying as this makes revision a much less formidable task.

For plays, brief notes on each scene will be sufficient. Here is an example, based on a few scenes from Shakespeare's *Macbeth*:

Act one

SCENE I *Witches:* they will meet Macbeth after the battle.

SCENE II *Duncan, Malcolm,* and *Captain:* report of Macbeth's bravery. + *Ross:* Cawdor, a traitor; title goes to Macbeth.

SCENE III *Witches:* the charm. + *Macbeth* and *Banquo:* greetings; three titles and prophesies; witches disappear; Reactions. + *Ross* and *Angus:* first prophesy true: Cawdor: a traitor. Macbeth becomes 'rapt', thinks of murder.

SCENE IV *Duncan* and *Malcolm:* Cawdor executed. + *Macbeth, Banquo, Ross, Angus:* Duncan's welcome. Malcolm named 'Prince of Cumberland'. Macbeth's reactions: 'That is a step On which I must fall down, or else o'erleap'.

When summarizing novels, your notes should take roughly the same form, except, of course, that you will be recording the main incidents and ideas that occur within each *chapter*.

2. FURTHER STUDY When your summary has been completed, you should make notes on each of the following: (a) *Underlying Theme* (b) *Plot* and (c) *Character*.

(a) *Underlying Theme* Most of the plays and novels you will be studying will do something more than just 'tell a story'. To understand the 'story' is only to understand the book at its very simplest level. Sometimes the actual 'story' may be unremarkable and may be summarized in a few sentences. Behind the bare events, there is usually a main underlying theme and, very often, there may be a number of subsidiary themes as well. The whole point of the 'story' is to convey a certain view of life which is reflected in the action and in the characters. Everything that takes place must be seen in relationship to the main theme.

In *Macbeth*, for instance, Shakespeare is not simply writing a 'murder story'. His intention is to show us how ambition can corrupt even the finest when it becomes an obsession. An important subsidiary theme in the play is the nature of evil. There are references to light and darkness throughout. Evil is equated with the forces of darkness. This is brought out by the peculiar blending of natural and supernatural elements. The supernatural symbolizes evil and is in sharp conflict with the 'natural' world and its accepted standards of behaviour. The conflict is resolved in the nature and actions of the principal characters. Once this has been understood the simple framework of the 'story' can be seen in its proper perspective.

(b) *Plot* An understanding of the plot involves a close study of the structure of a play or novel. A plot may be highly ingenious in that the author sets out deliberately to mystify his readers and lead them on to an unexpected outcome, or it may be virtually non-existent. Most plots are built round mental or physical conflict which may or may not be resolved in the course of the narrative.

The simplest plot has a definite beginning, middle, and end. The events which take place build up to a climax which may take the form of one or several dramatic scenes. At the climax, the conflict may finally be resolved or events may take place to prevent a resolution. Seemingly insignificant happenings which profoundly affect the course of the narrative may only be properly understood at or after the climax. The beginning-middle-end sequence may be varied enormously. When this occurs, you should observe how the normal pattern has been altered and what effect this has had on the central conflict.

A play or novel may contain one or several sub-plots in addition to the main one. A sub-plot is usually connected in some important way to the central plot: it may run parallel and eventually 'meet' it, or it may be in complete contrast so that the reader may read into it a great deal of implied comment on the principal events and underlying theme.

The play, *Macbeth*, has a definite beginning, middle, and end. At the outset, Macbeth is physically brave and morally weak as opposed to his wife who has great moral courage. After Duncan's death, Macbeth becomes more and more hardened to the idea of evil and is not troubled by his conscience in all the subsequent murders he commits. Towards the end of the play, the positions at the beginning are reversed: Macbeth is afraid of nothing, whereas his wife breaks down completely. Every event that takes place isolates the hero more and more so that at the climax of the play he is facing the whole of the English army alone. The great moral and physical conflict of the play is resolved after the hero's death when order is restored to the kingdom.

(c) *Character* The main qualities of a character will always be brought out in the action, in the dialogue, and in the effect the character makes on others. Where the action concerns a tragic hero, a close study should be made of his character. No hero in tragedy is wholly 'good': there is always some fundamental weakness in his make-up, a 'tragic flaw' which is responsible for his downfall. Macbeth, for instance, is too easily influenced, and too ready to believe in supernatural prophesies. His innate love of power and his latent ambitions may never have come to the surface if he had not taken the witches' prophesies seriously.

It is important to realize that in a well-written play or novel, the main characters *develop*: that is, they are quite different at the end of the book from what they were at the beginning. They may mature, or grow wiser, or become corrupt, or discover qualities which they never knew they possessed. Macbeth alone, fearing nothing, and prepared to face a whole army is quite different from the brave, highly-respected general so warmly welcomed by King Duncan at the beginning of the play. Similarly, other characters 'develop' in this play, like Lady Macbeth, Macduff, and Malcolm. Less important characters, like Duncan, or Lady Macduff are *static* in that they do not develop in any way at all.

Close study should also be made of the interplay between characters in a play or a novel. Important characters may 'develop' because they are influenced by others, or as a result of the conflict between opposing natures. Macbeth is profoundly influenced by his wife at the beginning of the play: it is she who persuades him to murder Duncan. She, in turn, is deeply influenced by her husband. Her troubled state of mind, her sleep-walking, and even her eventual death are the indirect results of Macbeth's actions.

3. PLANNING Your plan must be a close and accurate analysis of the question. In the column on the left, you should note down in any order ideas or incidents which you consider relevant to the question. You should then re-arrange your ideas in the column on the right so that they form a logical sequence. You must know how many paragraphs will make up your essay before you begin writing.

The plan and essay given below are based on *Macbeth*. Study them carefully, noting how they have been written.

SUBJECT Show how, after Banquo's murder, Macbeth's character grows gradually more evil, and his isolation becomes more marked.

IDEAS	PLAN
Macduff flees.	*Introduction*
Lady Macbeth's guilt.	1. Position immediately before and after
Murders: Lady Macduff	Banquo's murder. Lady Macbeth/ghost.
and son.	First signs of evil and isolation.
Witches.	*Development*
Lenox and Lord.	2. Lenox: open disapproval. Macbeth
'The very firstlings.'	and witches: 'sweet bodements'.
'Sweet bodements'.	Evil intentions: 'The very firstlings ...'
Banquo's ghost.	3. Puts this into practice: Lady Macduff
Macbeth's intentions.	and her son.
Interpretation of	4. Macbeth alone – Malcolm and
apparitions.	Macduff; Rosse on the state of Scotland.
'Full of sound and	5. Lady Macbeth: guilt; Macbeth: none.
fury ...'	*Conclusion*
	6. End: Macbeth and servant: the
	situation. Comment on 'life'. His
	death; the restoration of peace.

Though at the beginning of the play, Macbeth is entirely dependent on his wife for advice and encouragement, he eventually reaches a point where he is able to take decisions on his own. Even his wife is not aware of his intentions to murder Banquo: 'Be innocent of the knowledge,' he tells her, 'till thou applaud the deed.' When Banquo's ghost appears after the murder, Macbeth is the only one who sees it. His wife cannot explain his strange behaviour and thinks he lacks courage. But this is not so: Macbeth has become wholly evil and will stop at nothing. His comment on Macduff's absence from the banquet hints of his future plans. He is now quite alone. Lady Macbeth, so long his partner in evil, does not appear again until the end of the play.

This isolation becomes immediately apparent when we hear Lenox expressing open disapproval of Macbeth and giving the first full account of his crimes. But Macbeth himself is quite unconcerned about other people's opinions. He deliberately seeks out the witches alone. Far from filling him with terror, the apparitions he sees are 'sweet bodements'. Assured of future success, Macbeth emerges from the cave as evil as the 'secret, black and midnight hags' whose advice he sought. Now there is nothing to deter him from his intentions. On learning that Macduff has fled to England, he says menacingly:

> 'The very firstlings of my heart shall be
> The firstlings of my hand.'

Macbeth at once puts this into practice. Lady Macduff and her son are murdered simply because Macduff has fled to England. There is no justification at all for this murder, for Macbeth has nothing to gain by it. It clearly shows us that Macbeth has become an unrestrained and evil tyrant.

After this truly shocking murder, Macbeth remains without a single friend. Most of the lords who gathered round him have fled to England where Malcolm and Macduff are preparing for war with the help of the English noble, Siward. Rosse tells Macduff of the dire situation in Scotland, where

'good men's lives
Expire before the flowers in their caps.'

At the end of the play, Macbeth is cut off even from his wife. Lady Macbeth's mind is deeply disturbed as a result of her husband's crimes and her own share in them. She is so overcome by guilt that she takes her own life, whereas her husband is quite untroubled by his conscience.

With only his faithful servant, Seyton, Macbeth has much to cope with. Everybody deserts him; the English army approaches nearer and nearer; in the midst of all, his wife dies, but he has no time to give way to grief. Her death prompts him to comment on life which has been for him 'full of sound and fury, signifying nothing.' He goes off to face the whole of the English army alone, still confident that he is invincible. He wavers only for an instant when Macduff disillusions him, and then bravely meets his inevitable end. Peace is restored to Scotland only after the death of this 'butcher, and his fiend-like queen'.

Answer these questions:
1. Show, with reference to the above essay, how a grasp of the underlying theme helps the writer to answer the question.
2. What references are made to the plot? Explain why they are necessary in the above essay.
3. How does the writer bring out the fact that the hero's character 'develops'?
4. Would you say that this is an exact answer to the question set? Why?
5. Show what relationship exists between the plan and the finished essay.

Exercises

Instructions
Where relevant, the questions below should be answered with reference to any plays or novels you have studied. You should write essays of between 350 and 500 words and not spend more than 45 minutes on each question. The best way to divide your time is as follows: planning: 5–10 minutes; writing: 30–35 minutes; re-reading: 5–10 minutes.

1. How does the author arouse our sympathy for the main character?
2. Give a brief account of a scene and discuss its function in the play or novel.
3. Compare and contrast any *two* characters.
4. Give an account of a character's motives for acting in the way he does.
5. Show what relationship exists between the main plot and the sub-plot.
6. Discuss the function of the setting and the background.
7. Show how a letter or a confession changes the course of the action.
8. Describe the part played by women in the story.
9. Describe how the author conveys a humorous situation.
10. What effect have new arrivals on the plot?
11. Show how the character of the hero develops during the course of the story.
12. Discuss the main turning-points in the hero's career.
13. Give a brief account of any *one* important event and discuss the attitudes to it of *two* or *three* major characters.
14. Would it be true to say that the hero's downfall is largely due to some basic fault in his character?
15. In what respect could this story be said to be a criticism of society?
16. Show how the author prepares the reader for a big scene or a climax in the story.
17. What is the underlying theme of the story and how is it brought out?
18. Discuss the function of supernatural elements in the plot.
19. What is the essential conflict in the story and how is it resolved?
20. What use is made of symbolism? Explain, with reference to three or four events.
21. What are the author's views on good and evil?
22. Show how a seemingly minor occurrence has important consequences.
23. What is the significance of any *three* minor characters?
24. Would you say that the author is concerned more with thought than with action?
25. How does the author bring out human weaknesses and virtues?
26. What coincidences occur in the plot? Would you say they are convincing?
27. How does the author succeed in mystifying us about the eventual outcome?
28. How far are the descriptive passages essential to the plot?
29. Would you say that the lack of any plot prevents us from enjoying this play or novel?
30. What do we learn about contemporary manners and customs from this play or novel?